By Small and Simple Things

Inspiring Stories of Christlike Service

Published by Covenant Communications, Inc.
American Fork, Utah
Copyright © 1996 by Michele Romney Garvin
All rights reserved

Printed in the United States of America
First Printing: January 1996

01 00 99 98 97 96   10 9 8 7 6 5 4 3 2

ISBN 1-55503-824-7

By Small and Simple Things

Inspiring Stories of Christlike Service

Michele Romney Garvin

Covenant Communications, Inc.

Dedication

To my parents, George Lee and Pearl Tenney Romney, whose lives of continual service have inspired the compliation of this book and much more. Happy 50th anniversary, Mom and Dad. I love you!

Contents

PREFACE

As I have compiled the stories for this book, I've been impressed again and again that we become more Christlike by serving others, and a change literally takes place in us. The stories illustrate how lives are touched and daily miracles can take place when Christlike service is rendered.

It is important to note that physical miracles are based on the will of the Lord, as He sees fit to fulfill His purposes. If we have not experienced this type of miracle, it is not because we have done something wrong or are less loved. It is the Lord's decision who receives a physical miracle. Many times miracles are used as teaching vehicles, not as rewards for worthiness. If we aspire to these types of miracles, we have gone beyond the mark; for we know that miracles do not change people. The main objective of this book is to increase our desire to serve.

Each of these true stories relates to one or more aspects of service. When appropriate, the names have been changed to ensure anonymity. I am grateful for the help and cooperation of those who allowed me to use their stories.

This book would not have been possible without the support of my dear husband, Craig, and my sweet children, Charlene, Amy, Byron, Daniel and Tauna, who were so patient as they listened to the stories over and over. I wish to thank them for their love and support. I also express my appreciation to my dear friend, Linda Kay Leavitt, who was my mentor throughout the process of compiling this book and completing music and tape projects. Thank you for believing in me!

I am grateful to have been an instrument in the Lord's hands in gathering these special stories. May your reading of this book help you to realize that "by small and simple things are great things brought to pass" (Alma 37:6).

Michele Romney Garvin

The Miracle of Service

The fields seemed alive with adventure. We three young boys couldn't have asked for more. Dressed in "army attire" and armed with our imaginations, we were off to do battle. Partially opened soup cans filled with dirt made excellent grenades. War raged throughout the fields as bombs were dropped and dust clouds billowed into the air. The unsuspecting enemy had once again been taken by surprise.

My father had served faithfully as bishop of our ward. Shortly after his release, he was killed in a trucking accident, leaving behind a young wife and six children. My mother was 33, her oldest child 13, and the baby only eight months. What a tragic loss! Mother felt she needed the strength of her family, and soon we were living in Saint George, Utah, surrounded by large fields.

We found many hours of solace and enjoyment in these spacious fields. They, too, became our playmates. I was the youngest of the three boys and deemed a "private" in the army, so my assignment was to oversee production of the grenades. I had become quite adept at loading the ammunition into the cans; but on one particular day, in my excitement to launch the grenades, one of the cans slipped and ripped the inside of my palm with its jagged edge. I felt an immediate rush of pain, followed by a great deal of blood. I grabbed my hand and ran to the house.

After Dad died, Mother lived for her children, and she was a fine example of love and service to us all. Having a love for her ancestors, she found time for genealogy and even served as the stake genealogical secretary. What a sacrifice this must have been as she performed her work faithfully and still found time for all of us. Desiring to instill in her children the importance of service and that same love she had for her ancestors, mother volunteered her three oldest boys to help with baptisms at the temple. Our house was only a block and a half from the temple, so we were available at a moment's notice.

Blood was still dripping from my hand as I entered the kitchen. With fear in her eyes, Mother immediately began washing the wound. The cut was three inches in length and quite deep. I remember begging her not to make me get stitches. I don't know if it was because of my plea or because of finances, but I didn't have to go for stitches. After cleaning it well and putting an ointment on it, she closed it up with three or four butterfly bandages. She had just finished wrapping my hand when the phone rang. It was the temple calling.

They were short-handed that day, and wondered if the Fish boys could come over and help. Families from out of town often came to do temple work for a large number of names. If they didn't get the baptisms done that day, they often felt disappointed. I was only nine and a half, but in those days a person who had been previously baptized could perform baptisms for the dead. On that day, my oldest brother had another commitment and wouldn't be able to help. My brother just older than I was playing in a Little League game that night. I had really wanted to go and watch him. Looking at my freshly bandaged hand, Mother hesitated for a moment and then said, "Jon, when you get to the temple, tell them you are the only one who can make it today."

Even though I wanted to attend the baseball game, I obeyed. As I walked the short distance to the temple, I could feel the throbbing in my hand. Brother Edwards was the one performing the baptisms that night. I will always remember him because he was missing a few fingers on his right hand. When he raised it to the square, I could see all of his hand. I didn't have any idea how he had lost his fingers, but as I looked down at my bandaged hand, I somehow felt grateful for what I did have.

For several hours Brother Edwards and I performed our labor

of love. Each time we completed twenty-five baptisms and confirmations, he would stop and ask if I felt like I could continue. I told him that I could. I really enjoyed going to the temple and being baptized. After personally being baptized for 400 people that day, I dragged myself home exhausted.

When I arrived, Mother was a little upset. I had never been at the temple that long. She thought I would be gone for maybe an hour or two, but not all night. I could see the worry in her face as she glanced down at my soaking wet bandages. Quickly she gathered dry supplies to replace the wet ones. As she unwrapped my hand, her mouth fell open in astonishment. My hand was completely healed! There was absolutely no sign of the trauma that had taken place earlier that morning—not even the tiniest cut or red mark! We wept in each other's arms.

We had just witnessed a mighty miracle in our day. Mother took the opportunity right then to teach me of the blessing I had received because of my service in the temple that day, and the experience remains very sacred to me. Since then, I have had a special reverence for service. I know that had it not been for my mother, I would never have given that kind of service. Because of a gentle, persistent mother who provided her children with many opportunities to serve, the miracle of service continues in our lives today.

Jon B. Fish,
father of five and
grandfather of five

"An Act of God"

The blaring sound of the smoke detector startled me from my deep sleep. As I ran toward the sound, I glanced down the stairs and was nearly overcome with what I saw. The couch cushions from downstairs were floating on top of the stairs. The basement was completely filled with water. Deep, murky water. My adrenaline began pumping. I couldn't believe that everyone else was still asleep! Immediately my thoughts went to my two older girls, whose bedrooms were downstairs.

It was July 1990, and we had just returned home from a family vacation at around 10:00 p.m. We unloaded everything and got the kids in bed, then watched the 11 o'clock news. A flash flood warning appeared on the screen, but I thought nothing of it because we had never had any problem with floods.

Now, shaking off my paralysis, I ran to wake up my husband. When Lynn saw that the water was nearly to the top of the stairs, his first reaction was to try to get downstairs to save our girls. I had to physically stop him and show him that the children were all safe and sound. During the night, the girls had become frightened by the thunder and lightning and had come upstairs to sleep.

We went to our bedroom and looked out the window. There, in our backyard, was a lake of water! I could barely see the top of the trampoline; its legs were completely under water. It was rain that had caused this flood, and it was still raining! How much higher would the water reach if it continued to rain?

The east brick wall in our back yard had just been put up, but not the west wall. As it continued to rain, a river of water came rushing down the mountain from the west. It funneled through our backyard, hitting our east wall and filling all four window wells. The water then continued on down the road in a south-easterly direction. However, pressure from the water in the window wells was so great that it blew the windows out. Water poured in and filled up the basement like a bathtub. When the water reached the fire alarm, it went off, awakening me. Because the water came in with such power, it forced the door shut. Had the girls been sleeping in their bedrooms, they would have been entombed and drowned. We thanked the Lord as we counted our blessings that night, knowing that this could have been a horrible tragedy.

Since we didn't think there was anything we could do that night, we went back to bed, comforted by the thought that this flooding would be covered by insurance. But this comfort didn't last long. Early the next morning when I called the insurance company and told our agent what had happened, there was silence on the other end. Finally he said, "Beverly, I don't think this is covered. The insurance companies consider this an 'Act of God.' This type of flooding is not usually covered in an insurance policy unless you have specific flood coverage." We were not in a flood area. Ironically, the home that we had just moved from *was* in a flood area, and we had carried flood insurance for eight and one-half years. We were just sick! "An 'Act of God?'" I questioned. "How can something this disastrous be considered an 'Act of God?'"

Following this devastating news, we started piecing our life back together. Our oldest daughter, Arianne, had left her glasses on her nightstand downstairs, and she could not see without them. I think I finally realized how powerful the water had been when I started looking for her glasses. I went to the girls' bedroom window and looked in. What a shock! Their waterbeds were floating up near the ceiling! The fan blades from the ceiling fan had been twisted in a downward position because of the force of the water. I looked in that room and thought, "No way! We will never find her glasses now!"

Later in the day, as the water was being pumped out, we were finally able to go down inside the basement, and people in the ward started coming to help us get things out. By that time the water was about waist deep. Some of the men went downstairs and began pulling furniture out. Women were outside hosing dirt off other things and putting them out to dry. My husband was serving as bishop of our ward, and it touched our hearts deeply to see the love people had for us as they gave freely of their time and service.

The small miracles that happened during the day were amazing. On one of my trips into the girls' bedroom, for example, I reached over to get some clothes and could feel something floating by my feet. I bent down and picked it up—a black case with Arianne's glasses safely tucked away inside, in perfect condition!

Throughout the day, the brethren continued removing all of the furniture, most of which could not be saved. The carpet had to be ripped up; it was so heavy with mud and silt that the men had to cut it into strips to get it up off the floor. After everything was gutted out, we made a door out of plywood and boarded up the bottom of the stairs. We didn't have the money to rebuild.

Two years passed and still there was no money, so the basement remained empty. At one point, we received three different bids for the cost to rebuild. They all came in around $35,000-$40,000. It was money we didn't have! One of the brethren who came over to give us a bid happened to be our high priest group leader. At that time, we did not know that he had approached the bishop with the idea of taking our home on as a ward project. He felt that there were enough skilled people in the high priest group to accomplish this. So, after his prayerful planning, we were asked if we would allow the ward to rebuild our basement. I sat and cried. I couldn't believe that someone would actually want to do this for us.

Our ward brethren came in the afternoons, at night, after work, and on weekends, spending countless hours away from their families. The project began in the summer and lasted into

January. What a sacrifice during the holiday season—and what a blessed gift for us! Our children came to know what it was like to feel what true love and true service were all about. These people were not being paid; they were there out of love and a desire to serve and help us. It was true Christlike service.

Little miracles continued to happen along the way. The air-conditioning man in our ward was able to get a free unit for us. Those who couldn't give time wanted to donate money, and a fund was set up in our ward that the priesthood brethren handled anonymously. Money from this fund was used to rebuild our home. Almost everything was donated in the form of time or money. It was a true miracle seeing what members of the Church can do when working together on a common goal. It must have been what the United Order was like during the good times.

As wonderful as this service was, it was also a very humbling experience for our family. We had served others our entire life, and now we had to be on the receiving end. Lynn had served as bishop to all of these wonderful people who were now serving him. "Cast your bread upon the water, and it will come back toasted and buttered!" We can truly attest to that.

At times, it was very difficult for Lynn to have other men come and do for his family something he couldn't do alone. He had to learn humility as he realized that these brethren loved him and wanted to serve him. Lynn tried to get downstairs to help every moment he could. One day as he was performing a service for another family (he was in the stucco business), people were in our home doing a service for us. One of the men said, "You see, this is the way it should be. He's serving someone else, and we're serving him. Everyone is using their skill to help someone else."

Our ward was divided during this time, and I was called as the Relief Society president—a position that put me in our ward's monthly welfare meeting. I must have cried every month in that meeting, just out of gratitude. On one occasion I commented to the brethren, "Our children are learning what true love and service are because of the angels who are in our home. No price tag could be put on what we have learned. If someone had given me half a million dollars to repair the home, it could not have purchased what we have experienced. An 'Act of God?' Yes, indeed. There is no other way to describe the lessons of sacrifice and service our family was taught."

Beverly Huntsman,
mother of seven

Full Circle

"Ding Dong." There was that familiar sound again! We couldn't believe it. For the eleventh evening in a row, the doorbell rang, footsteps flew, and goodies were left on our front porch. It was Christmas, 1992, and anticipation filled the air. My wife, Dana, and I felt like kids again. We could hardly get our seven-year-old son, Jeremy, to bed every night. We all wondered who these secret elves were who had attached themselves to us. We hadn't a clue! Being new to the area and neighborhood only added to the suspense.

For sixteen years I had been inactive in the Church. Dana was a nonmember and was filled with rather strong feelings *against* the Church, stemming from her youth. When I married her, I wanted nothing to do with the Church. We did not discuss religion and the Church had never been a part of our relationship. As the years passed, there began to be a void in our marriage. Neither of us could figure out what was wrong.

It was during this time that I happened to be in an LDS bookstore. I am an avid reader and can easily digest a book in a couple of hours. As I uncomfortably browsed through the books, I deliberately picked up some fiction, not wanting to get into any doctrine. As the pages unfolded, this seemingly innocent book touched my soul. Stirrings of the Spirit that I had felt long ago tried to surface. It scared me! I didn't like what I was experiencing and wanted to run from these feelings. How could I even think of the Church now, with my wife being so adamantly against Mormons? However, reading this and other books became like an obsession to me. I made many trips to that same store and read everything I could get my hands on.

This Christmas holiday had been the greatest one we had ever experienced. We felt an inexplicable happiness in our home. We couldn't fathom who would so unselfishly take it upon themselves to treat us with wonderful holiday delights for nearly a fortnight. Try as we might, we had never caught our little elves in the act. The cryptic note enclosed indicated that tomorrow, the twelfth day of Christmas, was to be the finale. We laid plans. We designed our own basket of goodies, placed it strategically on our front porch, turned out all the lights, and waited. As the hour approached, we staked out the front door with great anticipation.

I had grown up in the Church, was involved in scouting, and even served as president of the deacons and teachers quorums. Graduation from seminary added to my list of appropriate behavior for a good Mormon boy. I followed the footsteps of many other nineteen-year-old boys and served a mission in the cold country of Denmark. It was during this time that I began to question my testimony, and it was a very hard time in my life. I completed my mission, returned home, went to BYU, and was married in the temple. Later, when things began falling apart, the testimony I thought I had was no longer recognizable. A divorce resulted, followed by sixteen long years of wandering.

Now, crouched down on my knees with my wife and son, peering out of a tiny window in our door, we saw headlights as a car passed by. Then rapid footsteps approached. The basket was discovered; giggles and whispered conversations followed. With a flourish, we executed our plan. I threw the light switch. Dana flung the door open. Jeremy ran out. We had done it . . . we had caught our angels red-handed! Laughter, hugs, and Christmas cheer were enjoyed by all. They introduced themselves as the Merry Miss class from the Lone Mountain Ward Primary. We later found out that many others in the Primary had also been our secret elves. With a different car coming by every night, it was no wonder we couldn't catch them. We didn't know that we were one of six less-active families in the ward they had chosen to reactivate. We felt that we had new friends and that we were loved.

This wonderful act of service was our first exposure to the Church after all of those years. Our interest was piqued. Dana began asking questions. My thoughts once again turned to long-ago suppressed feelings about God. Missionary lessons soon followed; hearts were softened and underwent mighty changes. Baptism and renewed activity resulted. Touched by the spirit of service, we began doing service anonymously for those in need around us.

Christmas of 1993 approached. A family with no employment secretly received the necessary money for a round-trip airfare ticket home for their daughter, who was attending college on the East coast. We were impressed to give money to another family for groceries. We found out later that the mother had lain awake all night wondering and praying how she would be able to feed her family. The joy we felt as we served seemed to fill our hearts and our home. We had a marvelous time leaving another needy family an entire Christmas on their front porch, complete with tree and all. The exhilaration we felt knocking on the front door, then running away for all we were worth, was a fabulous payday for the inner rewards we had gained. What a wonderful feeling to be helping others!

As I knelt in the lovely sealing room of the Las Vegas temple, I looked across the altar at the beautiful faces of my eternal family. Dana's face radiated the light of the gospel, and her happiness could not be contained. Jeremy's eyes were huge, and he seemed to be taking mental pictures of this sacred event. As I contemplated this wonderful scene, I thought back to that simple act of service given us by the Primary. Because of it, we would never be the same. Our lives had come full circle as we mirrored the love and service we had received that previous Christmas.

Gary Widdison,
elders quorum president

The Trough

"'We believe in the literal gathering of Israel and in the res-t-tution . . . ?' Oh brother, I will never get this one," he said with such discouragement. "I have all the rest of the Articles of Faith memorized, but I keep messing up on this one!"

"Come on, Kevin," I coached, "just a few more lines and you'll have them all memorized."

I had recently been called to be the Blazer A teacher in Primary. There were about six boys in my class, ranging in age from ten to eleven, and the bishop had challenged each of them to memorize the Articles of Faith. As an incentive, he told the boys that all who reached this goal would be treated to an "unforgettable ice cream experience" at the well-known Farrell's Ice Cream Parlor. The boys were thrilled! He knew the love boys have for food at this age. What an effective way to get them motivated!

I had a very normal class of boys for this age. They were very physical and rowdy at times, and it was often a challenge to get through a complete lesson and have them listen. Kevin was somewhat different from the rest, however. He was quiet and pensive at times, but I could always count on him to listen.

As I got to know Kevin's family, I realized that all of them seemed to be quiet. They had been through many trials, including poverty, and Kevin's father had been out of the country for a while trying to find work that he felt might be promising. The rest of the family was left to more or less fend for themselves. Kevin's mother was devoted to living the gospel and did the best she could to raise a large family on very little income.

Finally the appointed day arrived. Four out of the six boys had memorized all thirteen Articles of Faith. They were excited and very pleased that they had reached this goal. The bishop gave each of them a gift certificate to be spent at this wonderful ice cream parlor. Because of another commitment, the bishop was unable to go and asked me if I would take the boys.

I loaded the boys into my car, and we started out on this long-awaited outing. On the way over, several of them began bragging about how they were going to order the biggest, most grandiose item on the menu, and one of them said he was going to eat so much ice cream that they would have to roll him out. All wanted to go for the "Trough," which was the biggest, gooiest ice cream sundae on the menu.

As the boys were ordering, my eyes were drawn to Kevin. Though he was as excited as the other boys, he hadn't said much. I was sitting across the table from him and watched him going up and down the menu, studying it over and over. I didn't know what he was looking for.

Near the exit of the ice cream parlor was a large candy counter. It had racks and barrels filled with candy. Some of the boys had brought money to spend in addition to the gift certificate from the bishop. They were intrigued by all that candy, and while waiting for their ice cream, decided to check it out. After they had left, Kevin leaned over to me and said, "Brother Garvin, I can't seem to find an ice cream cone on the menu. Don't they serve them here?" I looked and couldn't find one either, so I told him I would ask the waitress when she came over. They did have cones, but they weren't listed on the menu. Kevin found out that a cone would cost about half the amount he had on his gift certificate. He asked for one—the least expensive thing he could order! I didn't think much about it at the time.

Meanwhile, the other boys came back and their orders arrived. They were engrossed in eating their ice cream and getting it all over themselves and the table. Kevin was working very slowly on his cone. When we had finished and were getting ready to leave, the other boys headed out, but this sweet young man stayed behind.

It wasn't until then that I realized why he had ordered the cheapest thing on the menu. Previously I had thought he might be saving money for another trip to Farrell's. But as we started leaving, he said, "Brother Garvin, could you please come over here and help me?" He was going through the different kinds of candy and I now thought, "This is why he saved the money! So he could get himself some candy!" Then he asked, "Do you think my little sisters would like this kind or this kind? And do you think my little brother would like this one?"

Now I knew the real reason. He had ordered only a cone so that he would have the money to buy his little brother and sisters some candy. I was so touched by his thoughtfulness that I almost wept right there. At an age when boys are most interested in more food and more things, he was more interested in giving his brother and sisters the opportunity to enjoy a special treat too! He could have ordered a far larger ice cream treat, but ordered the smallest in order to be able to share!

I have seen many acts of service and sacrifice, but none to equal that of this young man. Every time I think of Kevin and what he taught me, I am inspired by his example of Christlike love for his brother and sisters. And I am prompted to go and do likewise.

Bishop Kirk S. Garvin
currently works as a judge
for the State of California

"Blind Service"

The crowd was silent as they watched the blind girl walk to the middle of the stage. The roadshow had been a funny one up until that point, but what was going to happen now? Apprehension was in the air as everyone's heart went out to this poor girl fumbling her way across the stage. What was it she had in her hand? It looked like a dog leash, but there was no dog on it. How embarrassing! Breaking the silence, she spoke to her unseen audience. "How do you like my dog? His name is Chip. What? You can't see him? Neither can I!" The crowd, realizing that she too could joke about her handicap, sat back and enjoyed a good laugh!

Several years ago, I was called to be the Laurel advisor in the Laotian branch in San Diego, California. Kham came to our class one day, and I immediately became aware of her as she sat quietly. That day I vowed that I would love her just like the Lord loved her. I found out when her birthday was and gave her a tape of music. She asked me for my phone number, and has called me every day since she heard mine.

Twenty-year-old Kham was born in Laos. She is happy and smiles all of the time. She knows she is blind and is not embarrassed by it! She has a testimony of the gospel and knows she is a child of God. Because of her blindness, Kham missed out on many of the normal things children do while growing up. When we would have our Young Women's activities, the Spirit prompted me to know how I could better serve her.

On one occasion when our young women were playing baseball, I went over to her and asked, "Kham, do you want to learn how to play baseball?" She asked, "How can I?" I told her that I would be her eyes and help her. She is very tiny and looks like she is about ten years old. So it wasn't hard for me to put my arms around her while we both held onto the bat. The ball was pitched, and crack! Kham and I had hit her first ball. It was a wonderful sensation for her to actually get to feel the impact of it, and she was very excited.

Another time we took our group roller-skating. I was having a great time out on the rink with the other girls. As I rounded the corner, I saw Kham sitting by herself and thought how irritating it must be, sitting there with the loud music blaring, with nothing to do but sit. My heart went out to her. I went over and said, "Hey Kham, do you want to go roller-skating?" She asked, "How?" I said, "You don't have eyes, but you do have feet. Pretend like you are walking, and I will do the rest." When she got her roller skates on, she became afraid. I told her if she started to fall, I would catch her. Then I took her hand and let her actually feel how tall and big I was. I told her, "You have to learn to trust me. I won't ever let anything hurt you." I recruited another person to come out and help me. One of us got in front of her so she had someone to hold on to, and the other got behind her to steady her. Then we started walking ever so slowly. Soon we were actually skating, and the air was whipping through Kham's hair. One of the biggest smiles I have ever seen came that day on the roller-skating rink.

On another occasion we went to the swimming pool, and Kham wanted to learn to swim. I taught her how to kick her feet and move her arms. Soon she was swimming with more and more confidence.

When it came to domestic things, Kham was also inexperienced. When she was at my house one day, I had dishes I needed to wash. I asked her if she wanted to help me, but she said that her mother wouldn't let her help at home. I took her hands, and plate by plate, we learned how to wash dishes together that day.

Another time, Kham went to a dance with us. "Kham, do you want to learn to dance?" I teasingly asked. She was up on her feet in a second. I placed her hands on my hips as I started to dance to the beat of the music, and a happy curve crept onto her face. She let go of my hips and started "rocking"! The rest of us sat and laughed with joy at the fun she was having.

When I took my girls sledding and tubing in the snow, Kham went down the hill with another person. Then one of the girls said, "Kham, do you want to go down by yourself?" "Yes," she nodded with confidence. When we asked her if she was ready, she replied with a big grin, "I'm ready!" We gave her a gentle push, and away she went. It was exhilarating for her, and she wanted to do it again and again.

Knowing Kham's love of singing, one day I taught her some of the hymns so that she could sing them. Several times I have taken her with me to speaking assignments so she could have an opportunity to share her talents by singing. I said to her recently, "Why don't you teach me some new Laotian words while I'm teaching you the hymns?" She was delighted to do this. It makes her feel good that she can help me—and she gets a good laugh at the way I pronounce some of the Laotian words!

Whatever I said, Kham trusted me. She had learned that I would always be there like I said I would. Because of this, she now believes in herself. My meager attempts at serving her had not only changed her life, but also my own. I have often thought of the words I said to her that day at the roller-skating rink: "You have to learn to trust me. I won't ever let anything hurt you." Hadn't my Heavenly Father said those same words to me when He sent me to this earth? Even though I was more capable of physically seeing and serving others, Kham had taught me far more. She saw with her heart! I had so much more to learn about trust and service than Kham.

Julie Sadleir,
Laurel advisor, Laotian Branch

A Yellow Umbrella

"How embarrassing! Why did that car have to park right next to ours?" I mumbled under my breath. It was summer and my husband and I, along with our five children, had decided to go camping at Zion National Park. We lived in Las Vegas, Nevada; at that time there wasn't a temple there, so we decided to stop at the St. George Temple on the way to the park and do a session. My husband would go through the first session and I would stay outside with the children, then I'd attend a session.

It was early in the morning, and we had parked at the back of the temple to avoid attracting attention. We unloaded our family, then I got the bowls, cereal, and milk out and we started eating. I was embarrassed that we couldn't afford to eat in a restaurant, so I wanted to be as inconspicuous as possible. It was quite the scene with all of my little ones sitting on the curb, eating cereal out of plastic bowls.

Without warning, a car pulled up right next to us. "Oh, great," I thought. "Of all the places that car could have chosen in this big parking lot, it had to park right next to us." The door slowly opened, and out stepped a humble looking, elderly gentleman. He started getting his suitcase out in preparation to go into the temple. I politely smiled when he looked our way; he energetically smiled back, and soon we were involved in a conversation. He glanced down at my children, then leaned over to one of them and sweetly said, "Mmmm, those cheerios sure look good!" During the course of our conversation, I learned that this man was "homeless." He didn't have a home, so he lived in his car. I was shocked! The image I had of a homeless man was nothing like what this gentleman represented. Many times, as I drove the streets in Las Vegas, I saw homeless men lying on the street. They were often called "bums," but he did not fit this mold at all. He was very polite and related well to my children. The more I thought about him, the more amazed I was that a homeless man would be going to the temple. How wonderful!

Then, as if a bell went off in my head, I thought, "If he said those cheerios look good, then they probably do." I quickly said, "Please, will you join us?" He hesitantly replied, "Oh no, no, I couldn't." "Please," I insisted. "Step into our dining room." We both laughed and he relented, admitting that his only food the day before had been two cookies and a glass of milk. "Yes, I probably could use a meal," he thankfully observed. As I poured him some cereal, he pulled up his suitcase and turned it sideways to create a chair. He sat next to the children and talked to them, bringing a warm, strong spirit to our conversation. My children were infatuated with this good brother and enjoyed the experiences he shared. It was so special to feel his spirit and be able to touch his life.

As he finished eating, I went to my van and started gathering some of our food to give him. When he realized what I was doing he declined, but I put it on the top of his car anyway. I told him that we wanted him to have this food. He then excused himself for a moment. I wondered what he was doing, because I could see him digging around in his trunk. When he returned, he was carrying something in his hand. He walked over and bent down to the children's level, bringing a yellow umbrella from behind his back. Speaking to the children, he said, "I want you to have this umbrella because of the kindness you have shown me." He then turned to me and said, "The Lord has sent me here today—for breakfast, and for much more." Then he added, "I'd love to give you a hug, if I dared." I immediately said, "Oh, I would love a hug!" We embraced, and he started to cry. I cried, too. He said, "You just don't know what it means to have someone show they care!"

As I watched him walk toward the temple, I continued to

wipe my misty eyes. I reached down and picked up the yellow umbrella that had been so unselfishly given. As I popped it open, I could almost hear him say, "Every time you see an umbrella, I want you to remember me, and the impact your service had on my life."

It has been many years since that day, and my children are now much older. But whenever it begins to rain, I look at every umbrella and hold to that memory once again. As raindrops fall from the umbrella's edges, I am reminded of the sacred concept of service. The taut, silken fabric of the umbrella provides physical protection from the elements for its owner. Likewise, when service is rendered, it provides emotional and spiritual protection to the receiver as well as the giver. I will forever remember the vital lesson in love taught by a homeless brother's yellow umbrella.

Michele R. Garvin,
mother of five

Aching Arms

The words she spoke seemed to be aimed directly at me: "There is a special need for service dealing with unwed mothers." I couldn't seem to hear anything else our stake Relief Society president was saying. It was September 1980, and I had recently been called as Relief Society president. Many of the presidents had been asked if they would check in their wards to see if anyone would like to be foster parents to these young, unwed mothers.

The Spirit had spoken to me, and I felt very strongly that this was a service in which the Lord wanted my family to be involved. I approached my husband with my feelings and he agreed. We had three young daughters at the time, so one more temporary daughter seemed all right with him. Several weeks later, I received a call from a woman stating that she was from LDS Social Services. She was the head case worker for unwed mothers and wanted to visit with us and tour our home. Soon we were on our way to becoming foster parents.

About three days after our visit with the case worker, Jill and her parents came to meet us. She was precious! Eighteen years old, she had graduated from high school and was about four months into her pregnancy. After meeting with us, her parents felt good about having their daughter stay in our home. And we received a witness of the Spirit that she was to be our foster daughter.

During the next five months, we felt both joy and sorrow. It was a glorious experience full of love and learning, and a bond was formed between Jill and our family that will never be broken. After she delivered, Jill decided to place her baby for adoption.

This very unselfish decision was not an easy one.

One morning about two months after Jill had gone home, I received a phone call from her case worker. She asked me if I could help her out of a predicament. She had two newborn babies who needed to be picked up from different hospitals at the same time later that day. She was calling to see if I would be available to help. She needed me to pick up a baby girl and bring her home with me until the adoptive parents could be notified. I love babies and told her I would be thrilled to help out!

When I arrived at the hospital, I presented my credentials to the admitting desk and was led to a small, private room in the farthest corner of the hospital. As I apprehensively approached the open door of the hospital room, I caught a glimpse of a lovely young girl, about sixteen years old. She was sitting on the edge of her hospital bed, cradling in her arms a beautiful baby girl, a gift from God. Her mother and father were standing arm in arm, looking out the window at the majestic mountains reaching toward the azure blue sky, trying to keep their composure and be strong for their daughter. I was very nervous about entering that room and intruding on the spirit that was there. I felt as if I might be stepping on hallowed ground.

The new mother was cooing to her daughter, expressing her deep love for her, telling her she was going to have some great opportunities in life by going to an adoptive family—opportunities she might not have otherwise. She whispered that she would never forget her and that someday, if the Lord permitted, they might have a chance to meet again. Her final words to her infant daughter were, "If I didn't love you with every fiber of my soul, if I didn't know beyond any doubt that you were to belong to another family, I would never let you go!" She kissed the tiny forehead and pressed her lips against each infant finger. Then she passed her baby from her aching arms to mine, turned away, and broke into sobs. Her mother and father cried with her and encircled her in their arms as I left with the baby.

I cried all the way home for that precious little mother who had just taken her first step on the road to recovery. How difficult this must have been for her. I was privileged to have this darling baby with my family for two days before the case worker called and said the adoptive parents had been notified and would pick her up.

Again with trepidation, I entered a room filled with a mighty spirit, but this time a spirit of pure joy. The cycle was complete as the baby was passed from my arms to the aching arms of her new mother. Tears flowed down the new parents' cheeks, and I left the room quietly. Like them, I too was shedding tears of joy!

From that experience came the opportunity to become a boarding mother for newborn babies. For the next twenty months we housed newborns on a regular basis. What a blessing that was to us! Some babies we had only for a few hours, many for several days. We loved them, fed them, clothed them and cared for them, and experienced heaven on earth each time, gaining much more than we gave.

April Goodman Baird,
volunteer for "OutReach"

The Gift of Receiving

Twilight was falling, the headlights were still on, and a large crowd was gathered around the car, curiously quiet. Shattered glass and twisted metal lay on the highway. The wheels of the car were still spinning and an awful gloom filled the air. In the distance, a little dog was running peacefully across the road, unaware of the tragedy he had just caused. A woman lay unconscious amongst the debris. I was that woman.

All I remember is swerving, skidding, and then flipping over and over. The initial part of the accident happened so quickly. But as I flipped, time seemed to go in slow motion. When the car finally stopped, I was slumped behind the steering wheel. My right leg extruded from the driver's side window, bent forward under the car at an impossible angle and bathed in a widening pool of blood. Broken glass was everywhere.

The hospital became my home for the next four weeks, days filled with excruciating pain and endless nights filled with nightmares. The hardest part for me, almost harder than the pain, was having to learn to accept help from so many people. I had been through some hard times while growing up; consequently, I didn't trust many people and had not allowed others to get close to me. Now here I was in a most vulnerable position, and I had no other choice but to accept help.

I am a convert to the Church, and prior to being baptized had a very strong dislike for Mormons. Over the course of events, my eyes, and also my husband Gary's, were opened to the wonderful gospel plan. During our conversion, we felt an outpouring of love from total strangers. Because of my past, however, I remained skeptical. How could anyone love me when they didn't even know me? As time passed, we began to feel the arms of our "ward family" encircling us.

Just before the accident, I was undergoing intensive training to be a midwife. On the fateful day of the accident, I was on my way to deliver a baby. I had been so busy in my life up to this point, and now all I could do was lie in bed in pain. The next months were filled with many hardships.

My first night in the hospital was spent in intensive care. Three different surgeries followed. My right femur was totally shattered, and third-degree road burns covered the entire inner side of my thigh. These were some of the darkest moments of our lives.

Then as quickly as despair set in, the compassionate embrace of caring, loving people wrapped a blanket of warmth and love around us. Within an hour of the accident, our wonderful ward was in motion. Our home teachers and others were at the hospital with priesthood blessings and support. Friends took care of our son. It seemed our every need was anticipated and cared for. So many visitors, gifts, and flowers arrived that the hospital was forced to put me in a private room for self-defense! We gave away flowers to other patients who had none. Still more came. Gary slept at the hospital on a hide-a-bed couch throughout the entire ordeal. His loving service alone was indescribable.

While I was in the hospital, friends went to my home and cleaned it from top to bottom. They organized our library, which I must say was quite a challenge. When told that this had been done, I was deeply embarrassed. I didn't want anyone coming into my home and seeing my clutter! However, when I came home and saw the wonderful gift that had been given, the embarrassment evaporated. My friends had done something for me that I couldn't do for myself. I was able to leave the hospital because of our new, extended family. Women with whom I felt a special bond took a day each week and stayed with me. For eight weeks, ward members brought meals into our home every night.

Gary and I were raised to be fiercely independent and have

struggled to learn how to graciously allow others to serve us. Through this experience we discovered the *gift of receiving*. Service is a two-way street. There has to be a receiver as well as a giver for the circle of service to be complete. The Lord has truly taught us the importance of being gracious receivers. We have been the recipients of supreme service. When we learn to receive, we gain a better appreciation for the Savior's gift of His atoning sacrifice. It is our testimony that when Christlike service is rendered, if we lovingly accept it, we have then made real the sacrifice of our elder brother, Jesus Christ.

> Dana Widdison,
> midwife, mother
> of two

Missionaries and Shovels

The neighborhood was quiet and moisture from the recently fallen rain was in the air. Vehicles of different kinds came and went unnoticed. However, as one of the cars came to a stop and I saw its passengers, I was surprised and felt a strange discomfort. What were two young white men doing in an all-black neighborhood?

In 1979, when my father was killed, I started having doubts about my church. I came from a close-knit family, and every Sunday after dinner we would sit comfortably and have family discussions. We had been taught about God, but I was not satisfied with my life. I started praying to Heavenly Father and asking Him to lead me to a church that would help me learn and grow. I wanted to feel like I was getting something out of it.

One day in November of 1982, the missionaries knocked on my door. I was living in Los Angeles, California, at the time. I opened the door to find two very nice looking young men who were white, one of them tall, the other short. I felt their spirit immediately. They wanted to talk with me, but because of family interruptions I didn't have time. They came by to visit me on several other occasions, but we had continual time conflicts. This went on for about three weeks.

During the fourth week it rained, and half of the ceiling in my living room had fallen in. I had pushed my furniture to one side of the room because of the soaking-wet insulation that was all over. When I opened the door to the missionaries, they glanced in and asked, "What happened to your house?" After I told them, they asked, "What can we do?"

I looked at them like they were crazy and said, "What do you mean, what can you do?" They asked me if I had any shovels. Still in shock, I went out to the garage and brought back two. They took off their suit jackets, rolled up the sleeves of their nice white shirts, and dug in. I was amazed that these young men who were strangers would care enough to help out when they saw a need. They quickly put the shovels to work, moving all of the wet debris from my living room to the garbage in the back-yard.

I asked them who they were, and they said they were "missionaries." I wondered out loud, "What kind of missionaries would come off the street and do what you just did for me?" They responded, "We're missionaries for The Church of Jesus Christ of Latter-day Saints, or we're sometimes called 'Mormons'."

My next question was, "Well, what are you doing in a black neighborhood then? I've always heard that Mormons don't like blacks." They told me that was just one of the many falsehoods spread about their church.

I love to read, so when they gave me a Book of Mormon I immediately opened it and began reading. With the first scripture I read, something grabbed me inside and I couldn't turn the book loose. I read it from cover to cover in one week. My heart was touched, and a short while later I joined the Church. In looking back, I realize what turned my heart toward the Church; it was the service the missionaries rendered to me that cold, rainy morning. My heart was softened and my mind opened so I could receive the gospel.

As time went on, the members of the ward were warm and loving. I couldn't have asked to be in a better place; I felt an immediate acceptance. At my baptism a little white lady, about my height, came burrowing through the crowd all the way from the back of the room. She ran up and grabbed me and held on so tight. Her name was Edna too, and she said to me, "Edna, I feel like I have known you all of my life." That meant more to me than words can express. I felt then like I belonged, that we were all God's children no matter what our color. The two of us have been best friends ever since.

After I had been in the Church only two months, I underwent major surgery and was in the hospital for two weeks. I still had two of my daughters at home. When I was released from the hospital, some of the Relief Society sisters came over and helped me. I just couldn't believe the things they did. What amazed me most was that all of them were white sisters. I just sat and cried. I had never had anyone do such kind things for me. I have never forgotten how loved and cared for that special service made me feel, and I am always looking for ways to pay it back through serving someone else.

Edna Ellison,
Young Women's secretary

To Serve Him Is to Love Him

I was paralyzed with fear when I received that dreaded phone call on January 7, 1991. As I drove to the hospital I silently prayed, "Please God, don't let it end this way." My husband, Don, and I had been married fourteen years. We had been struggling financially and were experiencing great stress, and we had drifted apart. We both were just tired of our life together, and our marriage seemed much more work than it was worth. To compound matters, we also had to deal with our teenagers.

Several months earlier, Don had been in an auto accident. I was very upset but relieved, when I reached him, to find out he was fine. This time, however, I felt that things were different. I wondered, "Is the Lord going to take him because of the bad feelings I've had?" I didn't understand why, but as I drove to the hospital I felt that this accident had a purpose. I wasn't sure what it was, but felt certain that the Lord would use this experience to teach me something.

I wondered if I was so hard-headed that this was the only way the Lord could get my attention. In the past we had a good marriage, but in recent months we had steadily moved in different directions. When hard times began, instead of building each other up, we constantly found fault. I was once told, "You should be the guardian of your spouse's self-esteem." We had certainly fallen far short of this sound advice. With news of his first accident, a part of me started to soften, but with the realization that Don was in no imminent danger, my protective walls went right back up.

At the hospital, I found Don unconscious! He had been up on a ladder and had fallen two stories. I had no idea as to the extent of his injuries, and fear gripped my heart. I knew that people had been paralyzed or even died from falling just one story. I silently prayed for help. Why was this happening to us now, when we were having so many other problems? Though deeply frustrated, I felt something for Don I hadn't experienced in a long time. The thought of actually losing him cut deeply into my heart.

The next five and a half hours seemed like an eternity. Don was taken to the operating room for reconstructive surgery. He had landed on his ankle, crushing it, and his entire leg had crumpled under the weight. The bone was broken so severely that it protruded through his skin.

During the next few months, Don experienced excruciating pain. He was not allowed to put even the slightest bit of pressure on his leg. He was forced to lie completely still while the healing process began.

We were really struggling with this ordeal. Our lives were totally uprooted by it, and many changes were forced upon us. Don had to rely on me to help him with everything. Then, as I began serving him, our feelings started to change. It was impossible for him to sleep in our waterbed and still remain motionless, so I made a bed for him in the den. In this room it was very cold at night and in the early morning. A fire in the fireplace made it bearable, so I continually stoked the fire all through the nights in order to keep him warm.

Don couldn't tend to any of his personal needs without me, which forced us to be closer to each other than we had been in a long time. At first he was not pleasant with the forced intimacy. I'm sure the pain he was enduring was more than I will ever comprehend. However, the miracle that took place between the two of us was worth any pain that either of us would ever experience.

The more I served Don, the more I loved him. Feelings long ago buried were born again. And because of the many hours of love and service I gave, he also experienced a great change of heart. We didn't fall in love—we grew in love. In retrospect, I am frightened by the direction our lives were taking! I know the Lord didn't cause this accident, yet I am thankful he allowed us this opportunity to change. I have truly witnessed a miraculous change of heart in both of us. We now have a bond of love and friendship such as we never had before. I testify that the best way to learn to love your spouse is to serve him or her unselfishly. We have now been married more than twenty years, and look forward to the rest of time and eternity together.

Name withheld

Lasting Memory

I hardly slept at all last night! Continuously I reflected back on another time when hundreds of worthy Saints had volunteered their service to the Lord at the Las Vegas Temple open house. The words of Isaiah echoed in my mind: "In the last days, the mountain of the Lord's house shall be established in the top of the mountains, and shall be exalted above the hills; and all nations shall flow unto it." Every time I drove to Sunrise Mountain, I realized the fulfillment of this great prophecy. Hearts were full beyond measure at the completion of this temple. As Boyd and I sat in the celestial room with President Benson, the General Authorities, and the others, a sweet, reverent peace filled the room. Each choir had practiced many hours for this blessed event. Now their voices, mingled with heavenly hosts, produced an angelic effect that I will long remember. My eyes were filled with tears.

Another sleepless night, I tossed and turned as I relived some of these precious, fading memories. Had my time for this type of service already come and gone? Finally I fell asleep, and dreamed that I was pleading with the Lord to give me a little longer—to let me linger there in the temple with the workers and patrons a bit more. It was as if I could hear the words, "Bette, you must go on to your next assignment. My child, I know you want to stay, but there is other work for you to do. I will bless you with a lasting memory of this priceless service." I awoke with a start. The following day, I relived the joy I felt while serving as the first matron of the Las Vegas Temple.

The beautiful brides seemed to glide through the halls of the temple, and the sweet innocence that accompanied their purity was so refreshing. It was a blessing to be able to take part while each was endowed on her special day. What a privilege it was to help a lovely young woman as she prepared to meet her new husband. As she dressed, I often knelt to slip on her white shoes beneath her beautiful wedding gown. She was now clothed in the armor of God, ready to be sealed to her eternal mate, prepared to meet the world. Her life lay ahead of her. What a glorious day!

Today was going to be a busy one. I needed to get up and get things started. As I walked down the stairs, I felt the soreness in my knee. My health was not as good as in years past, and as I felt my minor aches and pains, I thought back to my temple angels. That is what I called them. *I saw a miracle take place each day in the temple. Those giving of their time and talents were burdened with different heartaches and physical afflictions, but the Lord sustained them as they served in His temple. The countless hours spent in the Lord's service many times took all the physical effort these people could muster, yet they continued to serve. They were weary, but not weary of doing good.*

The radio disrupted my thoughts as the newscaster came on telling about a famous hero. Thrown back again, my thoughts were of the "unsung heroes" at our temple. *Our secretary and office staff were incredible people. They kept everything organized. Supervisors in the temple were also a very crucial part of its daily success; through prayer and inspiration, many choice men and women were selected to serve in these very important callings. Countless hours were spent as temple workers and officiators sat preparing, memorizing, and serving. Love and kindness were always shown, and smiles were given away freely.*

As I began preparing dinner, I thought again about the times I assisted in the kitchen at the temple. The brothers and sisters there were always so willing. *The list of those giving service goes on and on: the laundry and the cleaning people, the engineers, the temple security, and the gardeners.* As I glanced out my window at our new yard waiting to be planted, I reminisced about the special "Value Garden" the head gardener had planted for me. *It was a large, beautiful garden with flowers of each color representing the Young Women's Values. I stood by this garden many times as I spoke to the youth. I shared with them the importance of keeping their values high so they could some day come to the House of the Lord, where they would realize that in the temple, "hearts tell us things our minds would never know."*

I rounded the corner in the living room and caught a glimpse of a special gift—a picture of the Las Vegas Temple at night. Its spires shone brightly against the background of darkness. I thought of the many people who sat waiting in spiritual darkness for their ordinances to be done. Not until patrons come and perform this service of love in their behalf can they enter into the light. There it was again—the word "service." It came up repeatedly in my thoughts. I offered a silent prayer, thanking the Lord for the opportunity I had to serve in this capacity. Looking at that beautiful picture, I realized more than ever how I would like to pay tribute to all of those who served with me in the Las Vegas Temple. How grateful the Lord must be as he sees his children giving in this priceless way that reaches beyond the veil. The cycle continues with each loving act. It is indeed one eternal round.

Bette Tanner,
first matron of
the Las Vegas Temple

Listen

"Don't go near that house! He's the meanest man on the block!" These could have been the words passed down through the years. When Rob and I moved into Grandpa's house, we felt his silent presence through the response we received from the neighbors. This was our first house, and we were in the process of buying it from Rob's grandfather. After we moved in and began feeling some of the repercussions of the past, I had many second thoughts. I had looked forward so much to being neighborly and becoming friends with all of my neighbors, but this didn't seem possible. The people living around us were now old and didn't want to be bothered, especially by someone related to "him."

Grandpa Beardshall had been a very stern and forthright individual. Through the years, he had said and done many things that had offended the neighbors. Once he cut down all of his next-door neighbor's hedges, which grew between the two yards. The reason for this, he later explained, was because "I couldn't see the cars coming down the street." Another time he asked this same couple why they weren't going to church like they knew they should. They were not LDS and were very offended. Needless to say, the best of feelings did not await us when we arrived. It took a child to soften their hearts.

When Spencer, our oldest child, turned two, he started playing outside quite a bit. Dick and Gladys, our next-door neighbors (the same people who had put up with Grandpa all those years), still had chips on their shoulders. They had only one son who had married, but he didn't have children. We later learned that they loved children and longed for grandchildren. As my little boy began playing outside more and more, I could see them watching him. Inwardly I hoped that we could become friends, but I didn't know how to approach them.

Then one day as Dick and Gladys were sitting on their lawn chairs, Spencer knocked a ball into their yard. As he ran over to get it, I froze. How would they feel about having one of Grandpa Beardshall's great-grandsons on their property? My fears were short-lived as I saw Dick reach down and hand the ball to Spencer. Gladys took him by the hand and walked him over to our house. It seemed like the years of bitterness had begun to melt away. It soon became a daily routine for Spencer to go over to Dick and Gladys' house for some "Sprite." And Gladys would read to him and play with him.

To help our friendship grow, I tried to continually be aware of anything I could do for them. I had learned that Gladys was a staunch University of Utah fan. She rooted for the Utah Utes and never missed a game. On the other hand, Rob and I had attended BYU and were died-in-the-wool "Cougars." Our rivalry became a source of friendship, and we had a good time rooting for our separate teams.

One Saturday, BYU was playing the U of U in basketball. As luck would have it, BYU won. I wanted to do something to commemorate our victory, but the day was turning out to be a very hectic one. While talking to my mother on the phone, I told her of the fun, ongoing rivalry we had with our neighbors. I had really wanted to make a blue-and-white cake and take it over to Gladys, but I didn't feel like I had the time. Like many other young mothers, my intentions were good, but there were so many things that fell in the way of actually accomplishing them. As I expressed this to my mother, she told me not to worry about the cake; it would cause too much stress on my family. "Just call Gladys instead," she counseled. But as I hung up the phone, I couldn't shake the gnawing feeling that I ought to do something more than call.

I recognized that feeling; I had experienced it many times. But still I questioned: Why would the Holy Ghost care if BYU won? Why did he so badly want me to acknowledge that fact with Gladys today? Couldn't the cake wait for a time that was more convenient for me? Besides, I didn't know if Gladys and Dick could even eat the cake with their health problems. I had just about talked myself out of it when the gnawing feeling came back: "Do it anyway!"

Later that evening I took over a blue-and-white cake. I left it on the doorstep, rang the doorbell, and ran. I hadn't been home for more than five minutes when the phone rang. I heard Gladys's strange-sounding voice on the other end. *Oh no*, I thought. Was she angry that U of U lost, and didn't appreciate my kind of humor? Meekly I responded to her salutation. Then her next words took me totally by surprise: "I wanted to thank you so much. This has got to be the most darling birthday cake I have ever had!" She must have wondered if I dropped the phone. I was dumbfounded! How grateful I was for the continual prompting I had received earlier that day. I learned a lesson that I have never forgotten. If we are prompted to serve someone and we don't understand why, we need to be wise enough to obey anyway.

Because of this one act of service our friendship blossomed, and through the years we became really close. After her husband died, we included her in all our family activities. Our children grew to love her and considered her another grandmother. Our lives were enriched because of our association. Her health went downhill soon after we moved to Las Vegas, and she died shortly thereafter. What a blessing it was to have known, loved, and served her. We are better people because of it.

Elaine Beardshall,
serves as Primary
music leader

The Ripple Effect

Have you ever thrown a pebble into a pond and watched what happens? The movement caused by that one little pebble creates a tiny ripple, which then creates more ripples. Soon the whole pond is transformed into a medley of tiny waves. The once quiet, glass-like water now dances with motion.

If a single pebble can make such a difference to a pond, how much difference can one person make in another person's life? It's the small and simple things—the tiny pebbles of service—that cause the greatest ripples for good.

It was the hottest month of the year, and there I sat in a tiny camp trailer with sweat dripping down my back. The compressor could only be used for a couple of hours a day, and I had already used my quota. I was miserable. I lived in the trailer because it was part of my job. As the large trucks came in and were loaded with dirt, I had to weigh them before they left. It was a job and a place to live. Nothing more.

The gun lay in my hand and I began fingering it. I had gone through so much pain, sorrow, and continual downfall that I thought there was no hope for me. I tried to come up with options but felt like I had none. It had been a long three years since I had left my family, my friends, and the Church. Suicide seemed my only way out. Yes, I would go through with it this time. Several times before I had planned to commit suicide, but had changed my mind at the last moment. This time, I thought I had nowhere else to turn. Looking out of the tiny window into the dark night, I could see the skyline of Las Vegas. Sparkling lights looked like tiny stars in the distance. I reflected back to when I was a child and remembered how I loved looking at the stars. Many times, as I looked heavenward, I felt peace because I knew Heavenly Father was there looking down on me. My parents had taught me that I had a Father in Heaven who loved and cared about me. Back then I was sure of a lot of things. Now I didn't know what I believed.

Absent-mindedly, I played an unlabeled tape from my tape collection. As the music began, the words of the song jumped out at me: "Will he answer me? Does he really hear my prayers?" I burst into tears, feeling the pain of my previous sins. Immediately I took the tape out and tried chasing those feelings away by playing some of the hardest rock tapes I had.

Later that night I still couldn't shake the painful feeling, so I went into my trailer and dropped to my knees. I spent the entire evening in prayer. I fervently asked, "Are you really there, or am I just talking to the ceiling?" I wondered if God could really hear me and answer my prayers. Somehow the thought brought comfort and peace. I hadn't felt that in a long time.

The next morning I decided I would go to church the following weekend. The closer Sunday got, the more nervous I became. The thought made me weak in the knees, but I got dressed and went anyway. I knew where the chapel was and cautiously went inside, sitting as far back as I could. No one seemed to notice me (or so I thought), and I sat there thinking this was a stupid idea. Why had I even come? There was nothing here for me. I got up and started to walk out, intent on going home to end my life.

As I was leaving, a young man about my age introduced himself to me as Steve. He said he was living with his aunt and uncle and working to earn money to go on a mission. He was very friendly, but I did not feel at ease.

Steve excused himself for a moment and asked me to wait there. Down the hall, I could see him talking to a dark-haired lady, and then he came back. He asked if I would like to come over to their house that afternoon for dinner, and we could spend some time getting to know each other better. I accepted and then quickly left.

Back in my trailer, I saw the gun on the bed. I decided to wait. Perhaps this person and his invitation was by some small chance an answer to my prayer. I put the gun away and waited. Steve came to pick me up when he said he would, and together we went to his house. His aunt and uncle were very friendly, and I felt welcome at once. They had five children, and since I love kids, we had a good time. I stayed the entire evening.

I can't explain what it felt like to be loved again. For three years I had turned my back on everything I had loved. Everything in my life had gone wrong. But now, suddenly, I felt new life. My Heavenly Father had answered my prayer in the form of a young man preparing to go on a mission, his aunt and uncle, and their family. I was still loved.

Steve and I became best friends. I helped him study for his mission, and we spent many hours talking about the gospel. We attended church regularly together, double-dated, and had fun and crazy times together too. I started reading the Book of Mormon and I met with the bishop. One day he asked me if I wanted to go on a mission. I was surprised that I could still go, and the thought of serving the Lord brought even more hope to me.

Soon it was time for Steve to move back home. The Lord had placed him in my life just long enough to help me get back on my feet again in the Church. Would he ever know how his Christlike love and service had touched me? Could I ever thank him enough?

After Steve left, I continued going over to his aunt and uncle's house for visits. I used their telephone to contact my parents and share with them the changes that had occurred in my life. Since I didn't have a mailbox, they also let me receive my mail at their house. A couple of months later there was a knock on my trailer door, and I opened it to see Steve's aunt and uncle with big smiles on their faces. They handed me a long, white envelope. The words in the upper left corner read, "The Church of Jesus Christ of Latter-day Saints."

Two years later I stood at the pulpit, a completely changed man, and reported on my mission. For the past twenty-four months, I had spent my life in the service of my Father in Heaven. Many lives had been touched while I served as a missionary in the England, Bristol Mission, including my own. We taught the discussions to a woman named Trixie, and she joined the Church. Trixie's friend, Colin, and also her daughters, Louise and Laura, were then baptized. There were many other contacts who changed their lives and accepted the gospel. As I looked back on my mission, I thought about the little pebble and the ripple effect. The Christlike love and service that Steve showed me had created a ripple in my life. I was amazed at the difference that one person could make.

Several years have gone by since that day. It's Friday night and I have a date. She is a beautiful blonde and sits rather close to me. It is dark and romantic as we walk arm in arm up the flower-clad pathway leading to the Salt Lake Temple. Before we approach the door, we embrace. As I hold her in my arms, I say a silent prayer, thanking my Heavenly Father for this precious, eternal bride of mine.

John

On the Road Home

I couldn't believe how long it was taking. I nervously sat on the couch reading *The Miracle of Forgiveness*. My husband, Mike, paced the floor outside the high council room where 15 men were deliberating our future. It had been harder than I thought, yet I could already feel the weight of sin beginning to lift. For a long time my life hadn't been right with the Lord. In the past I had become "hard hearted" toward every aspect of the Church. Now I sat nervously awaiting the decision of a church court.

Mike was a returned missionary and seemed to be the one most heavily burdened with guilt. As I watched the pain he had endured in the midst of our sins, my heart ached for him. I think that at first I had wanted to come back for him more than for myself. Nonetheless, when we decided it was time to repent, I saw new life start to brighten his countenance. Having reached this point, we had found the beginning of the road back home.

How did this happen? I had often wondered. We had made seemingly small choices along the way that had made a big difference in the end. After many years of marriage and three children, I had to face the truth: my life was in chaos. My first husband and I had been married in the temple, but shortly thereafter had fallen into inactivity. As the years crept by, I found myself less and less happy with my marriage. Mike found himself in a similar situation. It had all begun so innocently, but my friendship with Mike began to mean more and more. It wasn't long until we had fallen in love and his wife left him with three young children to raise alone.

It was during this time that my five-year-old daughter, Jessica, started receiving phone calls from Marsha Jones, her Primary teacher. She was the last person I wanted to hear from! Anything that reminded me of the Church made me hostile. I had been active while growing up and had attended four years of seminary. I had been married in the temple and tried to do what was right, but my life was still a mess. No, I didn't need the Church or want to associate with any of its members.

But Sister Jones was one who did not give up. She was relentless! Each week she sent a letter to Jessica, telling her what they had learned in their class that Sunday and that they missed her. I remember how Jessica would go to the mailbox every week, hoping for another letter. Pretty soon my daughter started pestering me to take her to church. Several times I gave in and dropped her off, then went back later to pick her up. At this point I still was not receptive.

After I divorced my first husband, my bitterness toward the Church continued. My poor visiting teachers—I really put them through the wringer. I soon got a reputation throughout the ward as the "meanest lady." I didn't care!

Mike and I finally married. It was harder than we ever dreamed, combining his three children with mine. We looked like the Brady Bunch, but we were far from the perfect family.

One Sunday afternoon, there was a knock at the door and Mike answered it. The elders quorum presidency had come to visit. I was at work, and Mike was preoccupied with building shelves in one of our rooms. He had on a carpenter's belt and was embarrassed to be caught looking like this on a Sunday. While I reacted with bitterness toward the Church, Mike never did. His pain was more of internal guilt, knowing that he had done wrong. Having served a mission, he knew the gospel was true, but it was hard to come back after having made so many mistakes. For this reason, it was just easier not to deal with church at all.

We lived in an area that was growing rapidly, and our ward was divided and a new bishop called. The Lord must have known we needed this man. He was a wonderful, concerned, nonconventional bishop who could relate to someone like us. Through a series of events, our hearts slowly began to soften. I think of the many presidencies that came by with cookies or any excuse, just trying to get in our door. Ward members extended their friendship whenever they saw us. Although they might have thought it didn't mean much, these little acts of service made a difference in our change of heart.

During this same time, we had devoted home teachers who were dedicated to our cause. When the wards were divided, Gregg Jones was assigned to be our new home teacher. Because I was working long hours, it was hard to find a time that he could visit us, but he persisted. As our hearts started turning, we had a great desire to know more. Each month Mike and I would assign Gregg a topic that we wanted to learn more about. He would spend that month gathering information and faith-promoting materials, then come prepared to present it to us the next month. A little while later, Marsha Jones, Gregg's wife, was assigned to be my visiting teacher. Slowly my hostility toward the Church eased and my testimony began to grow.

As I sat pondering these past events, I was startled by the sound of a door opening. There stood the stake president, a man of strength, a man of God. He came over and hugged us. He had spent many hours working with us during our repentance process. As he approached, I saw tears in his eyes. My heart was heavy as I thought of the long hours of service he had rendered in our behalf. I felt an overpowering love for him, almost the same kind of love I now feel for my Savior.

With trepidation Mike and I were again ushered into the high council chambers. We sat in those same familiar seats, unsure of why we had been called. My mind whirled back to an evening, not too long ago, when we had been there for a disciplinary court. After many hours of fasting, counsel, and prayer, we were disfellowshipped. We knew we had a long, hard journey ahead, but this time we were pointed in the right direction.

The voice of the stake president's counselor interrupted my thoughts. "Mike" he said, "it is with great pleasure that I invite you and your wife here today. The Church is always growing, and with the division of your ward, we have had to make some changes." My pulse increased as I anticipated his next words. Was I really hearing what I thought I was? "The Lord is very pleased with your progress, and he loves you. He would like to extend a calling to you to be first counselor in the elders quorum presidency of your new ward." We thought we would never again hear loving words like these. We shed unashamed tears of joy, and the sweet taste of repentance was on our lips. Yes, the Lord really did love us, and he had forgiven us. With the same joy with which I accepted my new calling as den mother, Mike accepted his new calling. Together we rejoiced.

As we began to bask in the joy of full fellowship, a question was asked that caused us to stop and think: "What was it that brought you back?" We pondered this for some time and then responded, "The love and service of key people in our lives who never gave up, even though we seemed like a lost cause." It is our prayer that those of you who are the key people in others' lives will have the faith and endurance to continue to serve them, even though it may seem unappreciated. The fruits of your labors, in time, may be harvested in abundance.

Name withheld

Angels

I did a double-take as I turned on the lights. My home was *completely* trashed, inside and out! I couldn't believe it. Everything, from clothes to broken toys, was strewn EVERYWHERE! From the family room I could see the kitchen, laundry room, backyard, hall, and living room. All were in total disarray. There were even crushed Christmas balls and decorations all over the backyard. I was so numb and shocked that I stared blankly into space. I was overwhelmed and didn't even know where to begin. Then I faintly heard the sound of the doorbell. . . .

For the past four months, my sister and her four boys had been living with us. Martha and her husband were in the process of losing their home, so my husband and I let them stay with us until they could save enough money to rent a place of their own. My sister's husband continued to work in Utah, and every time he would visit, he would bring a load of their belongings to store on our back porch.

Soon Martha was able to find a night-time job. I took care of her children during the day so she could rest, and also at night while she was working. She would sleep most of the day and then help fix dinner and clean a little before she had to go to work. With four growing boys, one of whom was handicapped, Martha had her hands full. She also had a lot of her own emotional problems to deal with, which stemmed from severe sexual abuse.

I soon began having problems of my own. Taking care of my three children plus her four, all under seven, took most of my time. Four of those seven were bed wetters, and I had to contend with piles of laundry daily.

I knew I had a major problem when my three-year-old

daughter became critically ill and had to have reconstructive surgery on her bladder and kidney tubes. She and I spent eleven days in the hospital. Before she was released, the doctor warned me against letting her play with friends or taking her into public places. Because her immune system was so low, going to church was out of the question.

When we came home from the hospital, my sister's eight-month-old baby was very ill. His eyes, nose and ears were draining. He was so miserable, and I was up and down at night rocking him. Out of concern for him and my daughter, I asked Martha to please take him to the doctor. This, along with the deep emotional baggage she was carrying, triggered her anger. She felt like I was trying to control her, so she rented a U-Haul trailer and started packing her things to leave. I left for a while so I wouldn't bother her. When I returned, I was not prepared for what I saw. As I surveyed the mess that lay before me, I felt absolutely paralyzed.

The doorbell became louder and seemed to nudge me out of the trance I was in. Numbly, I opened the door. There stood my home teacher and his wife. "Hello there," he said. "I'm sorry to bother you, but. . . ." He looked a little embarrassed and then asked, "Do you know why we are here?" He paused for a moment and then continued, "We had just finished eating supper and were going to watch a little TV, when we both were impressed to come see you." His wife nodded in agreement. "We got into our car, but instead felt we should take the truck." As he spoke these words, he began to look around. Having been in my home many times before, he knew this was not a normal scene. I could see his puzzled look when he glanced at the broken toy parts scattered everywhere. I started to cry. His wife wrapped me in her arms and said, "Whatever has happened, the Lord feels that we can help. So please let us." I briefly explained what had happened. They assessed the damage and immediately began working. We filled their truck with trash several times over, working into the wee hours of the morning. This saintly woman then took my insurmountable laundry home and brought it back the next day, washed and folded. As she handed me the clothes, I felt like I was standing in the presence of an earthly angel.

The story doesn't end here. One month after this catastrophe was over, I became very depressed. I cried at the drop of a hat and couldn't understand why. My house was clean, I had caught up on my sleep, my daughter's health had improved tremendously, and my husband was very supportive. I had nothing to be depressed about! In desperation, I asked my father for a blessing. In it, I was told that angels had been attending me, my health had been protected, and my mind made clear so I could attend to my duties as a mother during this difficult situation. But now it was time for them to leave, and I had to stand on my own.

After the blessing, I sat pondering the words of my father. Tears of joy came to my eyes as I realized that I had received service from both earthly and heavenly angels. Even as trying as service can be at times, I will never doubt that when you give, you receive so much more. Through this experience, I came to know more fully that my Heavenly Father is truly aware of my needs and that I am loved.

Name withheld

Pictures of the Heart

In 15 seconds, it was all destroyed! For the first time I knew firsthand what it meant to lose everything. We had a nice home filled with collectibles that had dollar value as well as sentimental value, and of course antiques, those delightful treasures which one works so hard to obtain. On January 17, 1994, when an earthquake registering 7.5 on the Richter scale hit our home, I began to examine what was truly important to me. What a devastating surprise it was to see all my years of hard work in broken heaps throughout the house. It was impossible to keep back the tears of shock and disbelief. But I clung to my testimony of the gospel for strength. I realized that it had far greater value than my antiques, and it could never be taken away.

With the light of day came a renewed desire to serve. As Relief Society president of the Northridge, California First Ward, I felt a great deal of responsibility for the well-being of the members. We had received reports from a fireman concerning the more heavily damaged areas, and my concern grew for several young families from our ward who lived in one of these areas. Realizing that I must search them out, I put on my walking shoes and started up the street. It wasn't long before I found them, with many other apartment dwellers, in a large parking lot, dressed in their nightclothes. George, Helen, and their two small boys were now homeless, and I invited them to stay in my home. When we arrived there, we found another young couple who lived in the apartments and had come seeking refuge. Within 30 minutes, others had also come for assistance.

We realized that our home was still unsafe, so we decided to set up a "tent city" in the front yard. Everyone in need could come and stay there. From my own family of four, we grew to a temporary family of 18—14 adults and four children. We took from our camping equipment a large eight-man tent and two smaller tents, made temporary toilet facilities, put the gas barbecue on the driveway to be used for cooking, and carried chairs from the back patio. We planned to use our food storage as a temporary means of food, until we realized that it was completely buried and we could not get to it. It would be several days before it was accessible. So we used the food in the freezer, which soon would be defrosted.

At the end of the first day, we gathered together in the quiet surroundings of our yard to thank Heavenly Father for protecting us. This became a nightly ritual for the rest of the week. As we gathered in family prayer at the end of each frustrating day, we thanked Heavenly Father for watching over us and asked him for strength to do the things that needed to be done. The feelings of love and unity we experienced will never be forgotten.

One of the children, an infant with serious medical problems who had been scheduled for surgery the day the earthquake hit, wore a colostomy bag and a urinary catheter. I experienced first-hand a young mother's love and willingness to tenderly care for her child while others patiently held flashlights so she could change the tubes. I witnessed another young mother's desperate search for a pharmacy that would give her antibiotics for her baby who was running a high temperature. It was very moving to watch how we pulled together in mutual love and support. I thought of what Christ would have done had he been there. Each one of us had acted as the Savior's hands as we helped to ease one another's burdens.

I was office manager of our nearby elementary school. It was my responsibility to go to the school to assess the damage from the earthquake and to help parents there with whatever needs they had. While I was away from home helping others at the school, the friends living at my home took over until I was able to get back.

In the days that followed, we learned to survive with help from each other. We made arrangements for some to relocate, while others made plans to start over. Nine months later, everything was still not completely repaired. It would take many more months, and the memories of that frightful day would remain ever present in our minds. I am most grateful for a kind and loving Heavenly Father who watches over us constantly, and for friends who love and care for one another in a truly Christlike manner. I now would trade my earthly treasures anytime for the heavenly treasures of service given by true friends in times of need.

As I read my journal and recall how "in 15 seconds it was all gone," I realize what really matters in life. My scrapbook shows pictures and words that can be seen with the human eye; but the real pictures of the heart can never be seen, only felt in the center of the human heart as service is given and received.

Doris Kilgrow,
Relief Society president,
Northridge First Ward

Remember

Gloria reached into her suitcase and pulled out a brand new red dress and matching red shoes. She had purchased these in order to attend church services while on vacation. "I really want to start going to church," she told to me. "I feel something very special about The Church of Jesus Christ of Latter-day Saints. If I ever join any church, it will be the Mormon Church."

My younger sister was able to attend church with me three Sundays. Then, the day before she was to return home from her vacation, she was killed in a freak car accident. A few days earlier, the topic of the spirit world had come up during one of our conversations. We had talked about it many times, and she understood that there was a life after death. On that day, I felt impressed to say something that I had never said before: "Gloria, if for some strange reason you don't get baptized before you die, *remember*, in the spirit world there are missionaries who will teach you the gospel. Find them and ask them to teach you and show you the steps you must take." As I finished my sentence, her face lit up in surprise. Her eyes were normally large, but now they looked huge, almost the size of golf balls. She then said these words that I will never forget: "Phyllis, if that happens, I will!"

My grief over her death was almost more than I could bear. She was gone so suddenly and it was such a shock. The only comfort I received was knowing that she would accept the gospel. Through the next year, I had several spiritual promptings that prepared me to complete her temple work. Exactly one year to the day, Tuesday, August 8, 1989, I went to the temple for my sister.

I arrived at the St. George Temple just as the doors opened, in order to complete her work. That morning I was baptized for Gloria and 15 other family members. I also completed all their initiatory work and then was able to perform my sister's endowment. As the session progressed, I saw movement up in the right-hand corner of the room. I opened my eyes wider, as if to see better, and saw a group of ladies dressed in white and in their bare feet. They were dancing around in a circle, making a joyful noise. I couldn't understand them, but I could hear soft music. I think they were singing. I heard it, but not with my earthly ears.

I immediately focused on a young woman with long blonde hair, and my eyes followed her around the circle. As her head turned, I recognized her. It was Gloria. She was dancing, and looked radiantly happy. It was as if she wanted me to know that she had remembered our conversation before she died. We had both remembered. I could see one foot being lifted up and then the next being put down, in a skip-hop kind of movement. She would dance a while and then twirl. All the ladies were dancing. I don't know if the others twirled, but Gloria did. Then I heard her voice, not with my physical ears, but clearly in my mind: "Thank you, Phyllis, thank you. *We* are so happy!" This entire experience lasted for about 15 seconds and then ended abruptly. I was deeply touched, but told no one at that time.

About two months later, I was attending our stake conference in the Las Vegas West Stake. A visiting authority was speaking on service and how we can serve our loved ones through genealogy and temple work. He said, "If we could only see our loved ones who have passed on, we would see that they are literally down on their knees, begging us to do their work for them." Then his next words sent a bolt of lightning through me: "Those of us whose loved ones have accepted the gospel, when they receive it, will actually sing and dance!" I sat straight up in my seat. I couldn't believe he had said those words! Being a convert to the Church, I had never heard this idea before; but I knew this speaker was inspired, and that what he said was correct. Tears of joy came, and I felt another confirmation of the Spirit. Yes, Gloria had accepted the gospel, and my service had been joyfully received. Now, many years later, as I sit in the house of the Lord, again rendering service to more of my loved ones, I think of that glorious day when I was privileged to witness service being accepted—and I remember!

Phyllis Horlacher,
serves as a temple volunteer

"Cherished Moments"

The porcelain statue sat unobtrusively on my dresser. It depicted a mother caressing her newborn baby, holding the child in one of my favorite positions. It was a "Cherished Moments" figurine from the Hansen Collection that I had long desired. Mounted on a wooden base, delicately inscribed, were the words, "In memory of Emily." A statue to remind me . . .

As my eighth month of pregnancy approached, I began to feel strange things. Up to that point I had felt normal. Then suddenly I could no longer feel that special warmth from within. When I look back, I realize I was receiving warnings. Several times I had gone to buy diapers for this new baby, but couldn't bring myself to purchase them. It was as if I knew I wasn't going to have a baby after all. Yet my reflection in the mirror seemed to tell me otherwise.

Tears came as I held this precious statue and my arms ached to hold my third baby. . . .

Upon arriving at the hospital with two and a half weeks left of my pregnancy, my fears were confirmed. The ultrasound showed no life. Sweet Emily had returned to her Father in Heaven. My grief was full, like waves washing over me, then ebbing and flowing and coming again and again. I had so longed for many moments with her. Now what?

It was devastating to know that I still had to go through labor and delivery, knowing what the outcome would be. I was numb and I wanted to deliver as soon as possible. I felt it was important to be alert during the next few hours, so I would not miss the only memory of my baby. The doctor and nurses were a great strength and gave me unforgettable service. One nurse actually held me and cried with me during my labor. Emily was born several hours later and weighed 6 pounds, 8 1/2 oz. Though no breath escaped from her lips, we knew that her spirit lived on.

Moments after her birth, my husband and I held our beautiful angel child. Words can't describe what we felt. There is something very spiritual about a stillborn. Being that close to a person's birth and death seems to make the veil very thin, and the spirit in our room was so strong. As I held Emily, I felt so much love for her. I felt like she was there and that I knew her. Looking down at this perfect, full-term baby and feeling her warm, snuggly body next to mine was comforting; but knowing that I could not take her home broke my heart. I wanted her to wake up and look at me.

I was so grateful to be able to dress Emily for her burial. My love for her grew even more as I served her in this way. When I fixed her hair, put on her tiny dress, her lace panties and shoes, I tried to memorize each delicate feature. I was so grateful I had been a part of her life for this brief moment. She means as much to me as my other children. When I look at the pictures we took of her, I long for the day we will be reunited.

Sometimes people would say insensitive things to me. "Did she take a breath?" "Well, at least you didn't know the baby and weren't attached to her yet." Or, "I know someone who just lost a three-year-old—that's a real tragedy." At first those comments pierced my soul, magnifying my deep pain and the sense of loss. Then came the sweet, comforting answer: "How could I have known her any less? One breath, one hour, one week, would not have changed the love I have for her and the comfort of knowing we will be together forever."

Enveloped in a wave of love at a time I most needed it, I was given overwhelming service. I witnessed the example of many who followed their hearts as they received promptings. I marveled as I watched sisters listen to the Spirit and reach out to meet my needs. Many times I didn't even know what these were.

A loving Heavenly Father placed me in an incredible ward that truly made me feel loved. Sisters who didn't know me, to whom I hadn't even gone out of my way to be friendly, now came with arms outstretched.

I had never experienced anything like this. I had done my token service, but nothing like this. I almost felt unworthy. I couldn't understand why they would want to serve me, yet I was prompted to let them. I was served in ways I would never have previously allowed, and I experienced a change of heart. A new desire came upon me—to serve with full measure as I had been served. For the first time in my life, I saw and felt the miracle of service!

Once again my eyes are drawn to the statue. It means the world to me. What an incredibly thoughtful gift. Did the sisters who gave it know what it would do for me? A small deed, yet so far-reaching . . . a reminder of the "cherished moments" that were such loving gifts. A glimpse into the eternities of the "cherished moments" still to come with our Emily.

Christy Gibson,
mother of three

"Suffer the Little Children . . ."

For weeks we had endured the valley inversion. Then, the night before, a storm had thundered in, removing all traces of smog and leaving a damp, earthy fragrance in the air. The children were off to school, and I was on my way to a weekly volunteer day at a shelter for abused children. Along with two other volunteers, it was my responsibility to watch the children. I always looked forward to the hours I spent there, and today was no different.

Upon arriving, I settled in with two bright-eyed brothers, ages two and five. We built a city of blocks, selected a car, and made engine sounds, busily pushing our way around our city. Scarcely any time had passed before a young mother brought in her whimpering baby. Almost before we heard and saw him, we smelled him. His odor was so strong that it turned an airy playroom into something more like an outhouse.

Mumbling an apology, the mother stated, "I ran out of diapers and had to borrow some training pants." The baby seemed no more than ten months old. Setting him on the floor, she continued to explain his condition, but not to anyone in particular because all of us were avoiding her. Silently I prayed that another volunteer would go to this child, and I positioned myself so that my back was to him. But it was too late; I had already seen him. As I resumed my play with the boys, the baby's filthy, tear-stained face filled my mind.

His body was small and fragile, and he wore oversized, ragged clothing. Most of all, I saw his blank and staring eyes. He didn't even have that look that indicated he was searching for someone to help him. His eyes were wet and runny. The unpleasant odor was nauseating, the whimper ever more disquieting. I thought,

"How pathetic. Please let someone else pick him up." But no one did. I heard the door close as his mother left the room. I continued to play with the brothers.

It seemed like an eternity passed. Then the words of a scripture crept into my mind: "Inasmuch as ye have done it unto one of the least of these my brethren, ye have done it unto me." These words I recognized as the Savior's, from the book of Matthew. Still, I did nothing. Ignoring the baby, I wiped the two-year-old's nose. The brothers were darling, cute boys, and they were very clean. It was easy to love them. The baby was beyond dirty. Dirty to me was children playing outside in the mud, but that wasn't how this child looked. Nothing about him was attractive, and I wanted to keep as far away from him as possible. Then in a strong, firm tone the message came again: ". . . Unto one of the least." This time the words hit home. And, as if an audible whisper, I heard, "Suffer the little children to come unto me. Pick up this child!"

Motioning to one of the other women to watch over the brothers, I turned to the baby. I felt as if someone pulled me to my feet and carried me over to him. On the way across the room, I grabbed a blanket from a crib, then, kneeling down, I wrapped it around him and held him to me. I found my behavior unbelievable. I walked out of the room with the child in my arms and tears in my eyes. I wasn't sure if I was embarrassed by the tears or my hesitation, but I didn't want the others to see. How could I neglect this child?

We spent the rest of the morning together, just the two of us. I bathed him, put him in clean clothes, fed him, and rocked him. He never once smiled during our brief encounter. During the following week I thought of him as representing all children who deserve to have their basic needs met—the simple things we all take for granted.

The next Tuesday, as I returned to the shelter, I went with renewed hope. I would love this baby and every baby that came in, whatever the condition. Within moments, the tragic news had hammered its way through my mind, and I was truly heartbroken. This precious baby boy had died the day after I had cared for him. Stunned by the loss, I looked around at the other children, whose needs were not as readily apparent as his had been. Through his suffering, the opportunity to serve had come. "One had but to listen, then do," came the words.

Another storm had moved in, and as it started to thunder, the words came again and again. "One had but to listen, then do." These were strong, loud, and definite messages. The challenge was to listen and serve. Again I looked around the room, searching each child's eyes. Only this time I was truly looking.

Kathy Carlson, serves
in the Young Women's
organization

A *Special* Garbage Man

"Seth, where are you?" It seemed like I could never find that little rascal. Where was he? Then I heard the familiar sound of the garbage truck and instantly knew where my little two-year-old would be. Seth was fascinated with garbage trucks. He loved to sit by the window and watch the men drive up in these big trucks and empty the cans into the back of them. Today was no exception. There he sat, mesmerized with the sound. Little did he know that he was in for a real treat.

This was an unfamiliar neighborhood, and I often noticed that things were done differently here. We were visiting my parents, and Seth and I were the only ones home this morning. As the garbage truck pulled up, Seth yelled for me to "Come see!" He was fascinated! No man got out of the truck this time. Instead, the truck had metal arms that reached out and picked up the garbage, lifted it overhead to dump it, and then placed the container back on the sidewalk. Sometimes it would not be set down properly and would fall over, spilling out any garbage that hadn't been emptied.

I think I was just as fascinated as Seth with this new technology, though it sometimes bothers me that machines are continually being made to replace the need for man. Then, as I saw some of the cans being knocked over, with no one to clean up the spills, I realized that even this was not foolproof. We were in the back of the house when we heard a strange noise coming from the driveway. It sounded like a scraping or dragging sound, but I couldn't figure out what it was for sure because I knew no one else was at home. When Seth and I got to the window, we noticed that the garbage can that had been on the sidewalk was nowhere in sight. I looked around and just barely caught a glimpse of a tiny, shriveled man hobbling down the street.

I couldn't imagine who he was and what he had been doing up near the house. That evening I was telling my mother the events of the day, and I mentioned how puzzled I had been when I saw this man. She then told me the following story that deeply touched me.

"Billy is a crippled gentlemen who lives in our neighborhood," she said. "I don't know how old he is for sure. It's hard to tell because he's all bent and shriveled. I would say he is probably about 40 years old. No one really talks to him because he is deaf and dumb. He lives with his sister and they keep to themselves. For some time he had been bugging her because he didn't know what to do with himself. He wanted to be of some kind of service to mankind. She thought and thought, then finally came up with this idea."

"Once a week when the garbage truck comes, Billy starts out very early in the morning. After the truck has picked up the garbage can and dumped it, Billy comes by and picks it up, along with any garbage that has spilled, and drags it up to the house for safekeeping. He follows the garbage truck on its route, doing this with every garbage can. He is out until dark because it takes him so long as he hobbles down each street. We have our own *special* garbage man."

I sat there spellbound. I was so filled with compassion for this crippled man—how, in his meek way, he is striving to bless people's lives with his service. The neighbors have learned to love him. Even though they can't communicate with him in a conversation of words, they try to show their appreciation. They give him drinks of water and little gifts periodically. But I suspect the greatest gift he could possibly receive is the gift of satisfaction that he is able to do something worthwhile for someone else. That is true service.

Name withheld

A Family Affair

"I can see it now, six members of your family on a mission at the same time! Wow!" We grew up with a very mission-minded bishop, so when he said these words we thought nothing of it. Looking back, we now know he was inspired.

There were eight children in our family. I was number six. As a girl of fourteen, I received an impression that I should go on a mission. When I turned 21, I still had that desire. My younger twin brothers, who were just about to turn 19, had always planned to serve missions. My older brother Phil, soon to be 23, had not served a mission; he had been out of the Church for the last seven years. My parents never lost hope in him, and our bishop said he knew Phil would come back someday, because throughout his inactivity, he had continued to pay his tithing.

Through the course of a few short months, a change began to take place in Phil and he felt a desire to return to the fold. He started attending the young adult ward and then indicated that he, too, would like to serve a mission. He asked the twins if they would wait for him so they could go into the Missionary Training Center (MTC) at the same time. In three months, all three were ready to leave for their missions.

We teased our parents about how they would now be footloose and fancy free. Their four oldest children were married and gone. Now their four youngest children would be serving missions. The new bishop, recently called to serve in our ward, asked to meet with my parents. "What are you going to do with your time now that all your children will be gone?" he lovingly asked. They told him they probably would just enjoy the peace and quiet. The bishop asked them if *they* would consider serving a mission. Their children had saved all of their lives so they could pay for their own missions, and they knew money wasn't a problem. After praying about it, they felt that it was the Lord's desire to have six members of the Sadleir family in the mission field at once!

After my three brothers left, I was to report to the MTC next. As I prepared to leave, I became very sick and had to postpone my departure date. The new date I was assigned to report to the MTC was February 14, the same day my parents were to report. The next eighteen months were glorious ones for our family. As we exchanged letters from one mission to the other, the spirit we felt was ever so strong. It was truly an incredible experience to be serving the Lord at the same time and in the same capacity. Our letters were all on the same wave length, and we shared in the joy of service together. During hard times it was an added benefit to have each other to lean on for encouragement, because each of us knew what the other was going through. Our lives would never be the same because of being in the Lord's service. We were already reaping a full harvest.

It just so happened that all six of us were scheduled to be released at about the same time. At the end of our missions we went on a Church History tour together. I had served near that area, and a family I had been teaching was now ready for baptism. When they learned that my family would be coming to pick me up, they asked if my father would baptize them. I called and told him to be sure to pack his white clothes. It was a wonderful way to end our full-time service to the Lord.

When we returned home, all six of us gave our homecoming talks on the same Sunday. Our older brothers and sisters came to support us and sang a special song. While we were gone, our ward had been divided. The two wards combined on that Sunday and we were given special permission to have a two-hour sacrament meeting, during which we shared some of our choicest experiences.

Ten months later, Phil was killed in a car accident. We were shocked and saddened by this turn of events. However, as we thought about his life during the past two years of service to the Lord, we were filled with a calm, peaceful feeling. When Phil returned to church after his seven years of being away, he wanted to make up for the wrongs he had done. We learned a great lesson as we watched him go through the steps of repentance.

On one occasion he was with a friend who stole an engine out of a car at a used-car dealership. Before entering the mission field, he went to the dealership and asked the manager how much it would cost for an engine. The manager looked puzzled and explained that they didn't sell just the "engine," but the whole car. My brother knew that, but still wanted to know how much an engine cost. When the manager told him, Phil wrote out a check for $1,000.00 and handed it to him. He explained that several years earlier, he had been with a friend who had stolen an engine out of one of the used cars in the parking lot. He wanted to put his life in order, and this was one way he was going about it. What an example he was to us.

At Phil's death, we were able to feel the joy of his life and gratitude for his change of heart. While on his mission, he was inspired to write beautiful poetry relating to the gospel. He experienced a total rebirth, and his death seemed to be symbolic of this. He had turned completely to Christ and had gone forward. We were no longer sad. We knew he was prepared to meet his Father in Heaven and would be able to continue to serve him. Now it was our responsibility to live so that we would be reunited as missionaries beyond the veil, and together serve once again.

Julie Sadleir,
daughter of Wilma and
Edward Sadleir

Losing Yourself in His Service

Music from the organ quietly soothed us as we sat in the chapel of the temple in Frankfurt, Germany. My mind had been completely at rest until President Johann A. Wondra spoke. Unsettled by his words, I quietly whispered to my husband, "Let's go!" We stood up to leave, but our stake president gently stopped us. "Don't you think the two of you should stay?" he queried.

How could I stay now? I wondered. I loved going to the temple, and we went every other weekend. The other two Saturdays we used for grocery shopping and preparation for my home preschool. I had ten children in my house every afternoon, Monday through Friday. With four of my own and six other very lively, energetic preschoolers to teach, I found that it required much preparation. I was also a visiting teacher and the Star teacher in Primary. There were about twelve to fourteen children in my class every Sunday and that, too, took preparation. Now with this new calling, I felt I had more than I could handle.

My husband, Eduardo, and I had been stationed in the military. We had lived in many interesting places, and this was no exception. Eduardo is a Russian linguist and also speaks fluent German, and I speak Spanish. Since every other Saturday was our day to attend the temple, we thought nothing of the special announcement in sacrament meeting—that the stake president would like to have temple-recommend holders attend a special chapel service, Saturday at 7:00 a.m. We would be there anyway.

Did the Lord really need our help in this manner? We were amazed when we saw that our name badges had already been made. How did they know that we would accept a calling as temple ordinance workers? The Lord knew what he wanted, but we didn't yet. Our group was divided into three. Some went with the counselors and our group with President Wondra. When it was my turn to be interviewed, I explained to him my situation and that I felt I couldn't accept this calling. He looked at me with love in his eyes and said, "Sister Trujillo, I see you are a very busy woman, but I feel the Lord wants you to accept this calling." I felt as if the Holy Ghost whispered to me, "If you want to find yourself, then lose yourself in His service." I couldn't turn down the Holy Ghost. The blessing that followed was beautiful. I soaked Eduardo's hanky as tears streamed down my face. I still didn't know how I was going to fulfill this calling, but I was now willing to try.

After the sisters' training session, I again felt overwhelmed. Many of my Saturdays were filled with tears of frustration. I felt so small, and the weight of the calling was great! Seeing Eduardo grow in confidence and experience the joy of serving was beautiful, however. My love for my husband grew and filled my whole soul. I think Heavenly Father must see us not as we are now, with all our imperfections and weaknesses, but as we will become— true sons and daughters of God with glory and light shining in our faces. I saw this so clearly in Eduardo and others. I felt privileged to be among these strong and pure spirits! After a while, the older temple missionaries didn't seem old at all; they were young and vibrant spirits who dwelled here in older bodies! They were such an inspiration.

Members from all over Europe, France, Spain, Holland, and districts of Germany came to the Frankfurt temple. We helped some of the first Russian Saints go through our temple. Since Eduardo spoke Russian, he was highly valuable to these Russian patrons and performed a great service for them; and his fluent German enabled him to help the German patrons. I learned to follow the session in German and felt that my assistance, too, was appreciated. It was a joy for me to use my Spanish, which I had learned during my previous mission, to help the Spanish-speaking patrons. The purposes for which the Lord had called us to be ordinance workers was now more evident.

As I served, I gradually learned all I was supposed to, and my heart was filled with joy! I soon felt I had truly found myself as I served my Heavenly Father's children and could feel His approval. I learned to love those around me and felt love and acceptance from others in a way I had never felt it. Eduardo and I began to look forward to Saturdays. We would buy our groceries on Thursdays, and I would work hard during the week to prepare in advance for my pre-schoolers. Somehow the Lord saw to it that everything that needed to get done was done. Our children cooperated and helped in the preparations. They helped look after each other so we could go to the temple with peace in our hearts, knowing they were all right. They too were blessed by our temple service.

It was a year and a half later that I found myself in tears again. This time they were not tears of frustration or feelings of inadequacies. They were tears of sadness and joy. Our time had come to leave this most hallowed place on earth. Here I had been loved like never before, and how I would miss it! I had gained much more than I had given. I found myself in the arms of a dear temple missionary, crying with all my soul. Feeling her sweetness, kindness, and love for me planted a lasting memory which represented all that I was leaving behind.

Now, sitting quietly in those same cushioned chairs in the chapel and meditating, my thoughts drift back to that day not too long ago. I realize how close I came to losing one of the most precious experiences of my life. The Holy Ghost once again bears witness to my soul that when you lose yourself in the Lord's service, you truly find yourself.

Beth Trujillo, serves
as an ordinance worker
in the Arizona Temple

My Slurpee Buddy

As I walked up the pathway leading to the familiar house, I saw that the driveway was filled with strange cars. I looked among them for Lori's, but didn't see it. I was on my way home from a baptism and was prompted to stop, but felt uneasy as I approached the door. Before ringing the bell I paused, thinking back on the first time I was here and how much my friendship with Lori and Keith had grown.

They had moved into our neighborhood and lived just down the street from me. When we first met we weren't immediately drawn to each other, but over time we became friends. I learned that Keith was a member of the Church but hadn't been to meetings for a while, and Lori was not a member. Shortly before moving here, she became pregnant and they started drawing a little closer to the Church. A few months later, they learned that Keith had cancer, and this too seemed to lead them a little more into religion and closer to the Church. Keith knew the gospel was true and wanted to know more, and they started asking more questions.

Through all this we became close friends, and my love for them grew as I empathized with them. I tried to put myself in their situation and imagine the bittersweet joy they were experiencing. Their joy came with the birth of a healthy, beautiful daughter, their sorrow from the news of Keith's rapidly spreading cancer. I began visiting with them more often, and we grew even closer. At one point, all Keith would eat were 7-11 slurpees, so I would pick one up for him and drop by unexpectedly. Sometimes he would want the slurpee; other times he was so sick from chemotherapy that nothing sounded good. We'd put it in the freezer for him to enjoy when he felt better. He appreciated my visits, and soon I was dubbed his "slurpee buddy." Lori and I became closer through this, and every time I'd come by she seemed to perk up.

Keith's health was up and down like a roller coaster. Many a night they thought he would not see the light of another day, but miraculously he would recover. Lori was feeling the stress of his illness and the burden of finances, and Keith encouraged her to keep going on with her life and to be strong for their daughter. They grew very close during these hard times. Keith yearned for more and still more knowledge as the veil continued to thin. He and Lori talked about the spirit world, and he had several conversations with the bishop which seemed to comfort him. Lori had many questions and struggled to comprehend that there really was a life after death, but the idea of it all brought comfort to her.

Keith's family was a great support during this time of crisis. They took turns staying with him and helping Lori with the baby so she could continue working. All were feeling the burden and their imminent loss.

Flooded with these memories, I pressed the doorbell. The door slowly opened and I was greeted by a dark-haired woman who I recognized as Keith's mother. I could hear voices in the background and assumed that they were the owners of the cars. I asked if I could speak with Lori, but was told she was at work. Keith's mother told me that Keith was in very bad shape and that they might lose him. I just stood at the door for a moment, then asked her to tell him that his "slurpee buddy" had stopped by.

I went home with a dark cloud hanging over me and talked to my husband about Keith. I felt as if there was nothing I could do to help him, and it was very frustrating. I tried to call Lori later in the evening, but she was still at work. That night I offered a different prayer for Keith and his family. He had been through so much. I could finally say, "Father, thy will be done" and soon fell asleep. About 12:30 a.m. I woke up. I can remember feeling like

I was awake, but not really being awake. I tried to go back to sleep. As I closed my eyes, I saw Keith, in pure white clothes, walking up a staircase. He said to me, "Tell Lori that everything will be okay."

I thought I was dreaming since Keith had been weighing so heavily on my mind, and I tried to shut him out of my thoughts. I went back to sleep, and not more than an hour later the same thing happened. As I seemed to awaken, I saw Keith walking up the staircase again. He looked at me and said, "Tell my wife and little girl that everything is fine. I'm where I need to be." It was so vivid, so tangible, I felt like I could reach out and touch him. I just couldn't believe what was happening, and I got up and started walking around the house to make sure I was awake. I thought over what had happened, then got down on my knees and asked the Lord to verify what I was experiencing.

I went back to bed again and slept for two hours. Yet a third time I saw Keith. Again he was in pure white, walking up the staircase. He turned, paused, and this time said, "Tell Lori and the baby everything is all right with me. There is a life after death." I settled back in, and had a peaceful feeling the rest of the night. The next day was Sunday, and I went to church even though I felt emotionally drained. In sacrament meeting, the bishop stood and said, "For those of you who were close to Keith and Lori, he passed away last night about midnight." I sat there dumbfounded. My mouth dropped open and tears filled my eyes.

I had to leave sacrament meeting because I was overcome with emotion. I realized that it truly was Keith who had appeared to me three times the night before, and that he had an urgent message for Lori and wanted me to deliver it. I couldn't believe this had actually happened to me. I felt very blessed and very humbled. Of all the friends he had in the Church and all of his family, why was I chosen? I didn't understand. Could my little bit of service, in the form of friendship and a slurpee, have really mattered that much? The fact that I was nothing more than a friend to this family, not even their visiting teacher, made me view service in a different light. The sincere acts of service we render, without being assigned, can sometimes have a greater effect than the positions we hold.

I walked to Lori's house and once again knocked on her door. As she opened it she was crying, feeling deep sorrow. We embraced, holding each other tight. I said, "Lori, I have a message for you from Keith." I then related the sacred experience. She pondered it for a while and then said, "Since I don't really know a lot about the Church, I have questioned life after death. This answers many of my questions. I appreciate this so much." We sat and reminisced about some of the things we had done before Keith passed away. "I can't tell you how grateful I am that you were receptive enough to receive this message for me. Thank you," she said as I walked down the path and the door closed behind me.

Peggy Reese, serves
as a visiting teaching
coordinator

Against All Odds

Kneeling, I quietly prayed: "Heavenly Father, thou knowest how hard I have tried to find a job that will provide for the financial needs of my family. Please show me what thou wouldst have me do."

Lately I had found myself on my knees several times a day, counseling with the Lord. Several years earlier I had become a single mother of seven, and in the early part of 1989 I felt overwhelmed with the enormous responsibilities I faced. My family was growing, and two of my children were serving full-time missions. Even though I had a good background in business, I did not have the education to match my experience or skill. I needed to go back to school to achieve this goal, and it seemed as if all odds were against me.

After several days of fasting, praying, and meditating, I received a phone call from a family member, which took me by surprise. "Sandi," he said, "you and your family have really been on my mind these past few days. I feel that we, your brothers and sisters, need to find a way to help you. I think if we all worked together we could help you go back to school and get your degree." I was overwhelmed. The idea was very exciting; but I was horrified at the thought of approaching my family with my need for their help to get through school.

As our conversation continued, the Spirit bore witness to me that this was in fact an answer to my prayers and that I must give it serious consideration. I again prayed, fasted, and researched the best course of action. I counseled with individuals who gave me wonderful advice. After a few weeks, my plan was ready for presentation. Creating the plan was easy compared to the next step.

The idea of "begging" family members to come to my rescue was almost more than I could bear. I put it off for as long as I could. Like so many others, I was full of pride and determined to make it through life on my own.

One special experience softened my heart and changed my feelings. It was a necessary part of the plan to approach my bishop to see if the Church could provide the commodities I would need while getting my degree. As I struggled emotionally during my visit with the bishop, the sweetest spirit filled the room and he spoke words that were like manna to my soul: "I am so grateful that you are giving me an opportunity to serve you. If we do not have people to serve, or if people will not take our service, how can we fulfill the commandment to serve one another? Are any of us ever in such an independent position that, within a heartbeat or moment, we could not be in the position of need? Oh dear sister, it will be a joy and a privilege to serve you and your family in this noble and good cause." The bishop had opened my eyes, and I had been taught a valuable lesson on the true spirit of service.

Now it was time to approach my family. I decided to send a letter with an enclosed "contract" that first explained my situation and desire, then gave them an opportunity to participate by gift, grant, or loan. I agreed to pay back, as the lender deemed desirable, any money that was contracted as a loan. The response was greater than expected. With but one exception, every letter was answered. A few could only make a one-time "gift," which I so deeply appreciated. Most offered an on-going "grant" for the period of time needed. And one offered a considerable loan with a principle-only payback agreement. Words are totally inadequate to express the feelings of gratitude and love the children and I experienced.

The blessings continued. A single-adult ward in our stake became aware of our situation and offered to support my two missionaries for the remainder of their missions. The ward in which we lived literally "adopted" our family and nourished us with gifts and care as Christmas approached. And I was able to get a grant that paid for most of my schooling.

For one full year, from June 1989 to 1990, all of my financial needs were met by those who found joy in service, even those for whom it was a hardship. One family even cashed in their life-insurance policy and sent the money to me.

As a result of this incredible service, my family and I became more considerate of each other, felt closer and worked better together, and determined to always make ourselves available to others when service was needed. I was able to complete my degree and, after graduation, find a suitable job that allowed me to meet the financial obligations of my large family. This short-term, intense dedication from so many created a long-term, successful solution to a severe family problem.

As a humble daughter of Heavenly Father, I express my eternal gratitude. My heart is filled with love for these caring, Christlike people who served me and my children so unselfishly. I am deeply thankful to Heavenly Father for answering my many pleas for help.

Sandi Reid, serves
as Relief Society president

My Brother's Keeper

We locked our car doors, then cautiously rolled down the window a crack to hear what the man was saying. "Please," he said, "we need a ride. My wife is very ill. Please, will you help us?" As we drove, his words kept echoing in my mind.

My husband and I and our baby daughter had been shopping and were coming home from the store. The weather was extremely windy and cold, but the warmth of our car was very comforting. We were in the right lane at a red light and were slowly moving up as the cars in front of us turned right. As we approached the intersection, we saw an elderly man standing at the corner. We could see he was saying something to each car that passed him, but our windows were rolled up and we could not hear him. We rolled them down when we got closer to him, then stopped so we could hear what he was saying.

"Please, will you help us?" His pleadings for help had seemed so convincing. Filled with mixed emotions about whether to help this man, we hesitated at the red light. We had seen so many homeless people with signs requesting money, or help in some way. Was this man's request legitimate? Fear of possible danger from helping a stranger engulfed us. My husband and I looked at each other and then we rolled up our window. Where was this man's wife? We both looked around trying to find her.

It was just as we thought. There was no one else out in this horrible weather. What did he take us for, anyway? When we were about ready to drive away, a thought came to mind, "Am I my brother's keeper?" I couldn't ignore it. Then I felt an overwhelming surge of charity. We didn't offer an audible prayer, but it was as if in our hearts we prayed, "Father, if this is what thou wouldst have us do, please protect us and our little baby in the back seat!" Then, turning toward each other, we knew what to do.

"Where is your wife?" we asked the weather-beaten man. As soon as he heard our question, he immediately cried, "Thank you God. Oh, God bless you. Thank you, thank you!" I glanced at my husband and a new warmth filled our car. As I turned back to speak to this man, he was gone. Looking down the street, we could see the shadow of an overly exhausted man running toward something. We quickly followed him as we offered one more silent prayer for protection.

There, up the street about a block away, was a very sick-looking little old lady huddled in her blankets, trying to stay out of the wind and keep warm. Her husband ran to her and helped her up with great care. We unlocked our back doors for them to get in. When the woman sat down and leaned back against the seat, a smile illuminated her tired face. Her husband was filled with such deep gratitude. "Thank you so much. God bless you," he repeated over and over.

As we drove them to their apartment, we learned that they had spent the entire day at the hospital getting treatment for his sick wife. Their car was in the shop getting new brakes and so they had walked, but she was too sick to go any further. Because they were trying to keep her out of the direct wind, they were not standing by the bus stop, and the bus had passed them by several times.

When we arrived at their apartment, we helped this little couple out of the car. Once again this appreciative man showered us with gratitude. "God bless you, God bless you." As we drove away, I cried all the way home, his words playing over and over in my mind. Amidst the hustle and bustle of everyday living, we had found our brother. Later I came upon a quote from President Spencer W. Kimball that summed up what happened on that cold, windy night: "The Lord answers our prayers, but it is usually through another person that he meets our needs."

Am I my brother's keeper? The answer rang out clearly to me, "Yes indeed!"

Tonya Larsen, serves in
Young Women's program

"Christmas Gift"

Christmas morning wasn't complete until after the phone rang! Mother would run to answer it with great anticipation. Breathlessly she would pick up the receiver just in time to hear my grandmother say, "Christmas Gift!" Then mother would say, "Oh, you won again. I know, I owe you!" Some tradition! The last person to say "Christmas Gift" was supposed to give the other a gift. A silly tradition, I thought then. It never really made much sense to me. Until Friday, December 18, 1992. That day I learned what the phrase "Christmas Gift" really meant.

It had rained the night before, and more rain was expected throughout the day. As a school teacher, I dreaded a day like this. It added to the students' excitement, making them extremely hyperactive. The day started off poorly and, because of other problems, got continually worse. So much for "peace on earth, good will towards men," I thought.

By the time school was dismissed, I was in a less than cheerful, festive mood. It was still drizzling outside, and I was feeling extremely negative. The last thing I wanted to do was drive fifteen miles out in the country and feed the migrant workers from Mexico and Central America, as my roommate and I had planned.

Two other public school teachers, my roommate, and I had decided that instead of exchanging gifts this Christmas, we would take the money we would have spent on each other, go to a thrift store, and buy clothes for the migrant workers. We would then go out with Paz de Christo, help feed them, and give them the clothing.

Several weeks earlier, the four of us had met at a store and purchased three grocery carts full of clothing. Then my roommate had started another job and was in Los Angeles at a training seminar, so she couldn't go. The other two needed to pick up a school van to take some students with us to help serve the food. We all arranged to meet at the orchards. But what had sounded like an altruistic idea at the time now sounded terrible. All I wanted to do was go home and hide from the world. The last thing I wanted to do was stand out in the mud and rain and feed homeless workers a meal that was usually so bad that I considered it unfit to feed to my dog. However, I felt duty-bound.

I hurriedly drove home, changed my clothes, grabbed our donations, and drove out to the orchards in Higley, Arizona. When I arrived, I was surprised by the number of migrant workers I saw there. Already my two friends and some of the students from Mesa High were beginning to hand out some of the things we had purchased earlier. "Father Tim" was in charge and had his food van nearby. A few other students were handing out plastic garbage sacks to the people to use as raincoats.

The immigrants had formed a line along the trees and seemed anxious to be fed. As I approached Father Tim, he said, "This guy first. He really needs a coat." I told him I had one and ran to my car to get one of the coats I had brought. Father Tim caught me on the way back to make sure the coat was to be donated, not just borrowed. I assured him that I had brought them to give away, and he told me to give one to the man in the van. He had just arrived from Guatemala and was in very bad shape.

I looked through the side door of the van to see a man in his late forties or early fifties huddled over, sitting on some of the empty food containers. He was soaking wet and shivering and just generally looked miserable. But what attracted my attention most were his feet. He had no shoes! And his feet looked awful. At that moment I finally believed what Father Tim had told us. Some of these people, he said, had actually walked barefoot from Central America to get to the orchards to earn money. The appearance of this man's feet proved the claim was not an exaggeration. They were callused, but still bruised and infected, and there was mud in the open sores. It must have been excruciat-ingly painful to walk all that way, I thought.

I leaned into the van and handed the man one of the coats—the big, soft one—which he immediately grasped and put on. It was much too big for his small frame, and I asked one of the bilingual men to ask him if he would prefer a smaller coat. In reply the man folded his arms to his chest, clutching the coat close to his body, looked me in the eye and smiled the most beau-tiful, nearly toothless smile I've ever seen. Into my mind came the words of my grandmother, perfectly clear: *"Christmas Gift."* The moment was so sweet it brought tears to my eyes. I smiled back and then took a position in the line to serve food. We were still serving well after dark.

Because it was the holiday season, people had been generous in their donations. After the immigrants had eaten, blankets were given out to the new people who had just arrived that day. I helped hand out samples of toothbrushes, toothpaste, deodorant, socks, and other personal necessities.

When our work was finished, we spontaneously formed a cir-cle and began singing Christmas carols. One of the cars had its lights on, and we could see the rain falling lightly. In our circle were two Catholic priests, a couple from Poland who spoke lim-ited English, a Hindu student, a worker from Mexico and myself, the only Mormon. Someone had brought some candles and by holding one of our hands over the flame, we could keep the rain from extinguishing the fire and also warm our hands. About fifty feet away, in a clearing, some of the workers had made a small bonfire. As we sang "Silent Night," "O Come, O Come Emmanuel," and "He ain't Heavy, He's my Brother," it occurred to me that this is what true Christianity is all about—Christlike service.

It's about having little, but sharing it. It's about being one in purpose in order to serve those who stand in need, without concern for nationality, ethnic background, or religious denomination. It's about forgetting yourself in order to give of yourself. It's about losing yourself and truly finding yourself. Grandma would be so proud, I thought, for I have discovered the greatest "Christmas Gift" of all!

Name withheld

My Brownies Made a Difference

I was exhausted! Being a single parent and providing our only income required that I work afternoons and evenings to try to make ends meet. My three children and I had been living in a tiny apartment, and I had finally found a larger one that I could afford. Because of my work schedule, I had limited time to make this move. At first I felt very overwhelmed trying to do all this by myself. One morning I was pleasantly surprised when four volunteers—sisters from my ward Relief Society—came to my door. One was my visiting teacher and another was the Relief Society president. As we worked together, I felt a surge of hope and great strength. They were so helpful, and I deeply appreciated their timely efforts. That very day, I vowed that I would do something for each of these women to show my gratitude, even if it was just a little note or a plate of cookies.

Soon we were in our new home, and I was running again at full speed. I often thought back to that reassuring feeling of strength I had felt when those sisters were helping me, and I was continually reminded of the vow I had made that day. However, the more I tried to find the time to make these sisters something, the harder it became. The adversary had almost convinced me that as a single parent, I just couldn't take time out of my extremely busy schedule. It was so difficult to fit anything extra into my life. So I kept procrastinating.

One Saturday morning, I awoke with a full list of things to accomplish. Then an overwhelming feeling came over me. As I started down my list of things to do, I couldn't continue. I felt a distinct impression that I should take that day to do something to thank those dear sisters who had helped me move. Part of me kept thinking, "But I need to do these other things . . . why today? I've waited this long; what's another day or two going to matter?" But the feeling lingered. "Don't put it off anymore! Get it done today."

I knew that I was not going to feel good until I got this done, so I quickly set to work. I decided to mix up a relatively easy recipe of chocolate brownies, but it was trouble from the beginning. One batch was over-done because my oven cooked hotter than normal, and the recipe did not produce as many brownies as it said it would. Money was very tight and I could not afford to get more groceries until next payday. So when I ran out of eggs, that quickly ended the making of any more brownies.

Then I turned to see my daughters eating the only few decent brownies I did have. I was so frustrated that I felt like throwing them all in the trash and counting this as one of my stupid ideas. The adversary had a heyday with me, and I allowed him to discourage me for a while. I felt worthless and inadequate. What made me think these ladies would want such horrible looking brownies? "No, I'm not going to take these to them," I thought. "It won't make a difference anyway." The adversary had almost won. Then that same little feeling nudged its way ever so slightly into my heart once again: "Go ahead and do it, even if there are only six brownies on each plate. It's the thought that counts!"

With faith like that of a child, I obeyed. I placed six over-done brownies on each plate, covered them with saran wrap, and tied a ribbon around each package, trying to make my burnt offering look as presentable as possible. Hesitantly I took these plates to each of the four ladies. As I handed them my meager gift, I was appropriately thanked. However, Peggy, our Relief Society president, gave me a somewhat puzzled look, as if her thoughts were somewhere else. I felt as if I had interrupted her, and she was having trouble changing her train of thought, so I quickly exchanged pleasantries with her and left.

On the way home, even though I was puzzled by Peggy's response, I felt a sense of satisfaction. Grateful that I had been able in some way to say "thank you," I was able to walk a little taller that day. I knew those brownies wouldn't matter much to those sisters, although they had to me. But I was very wrong. It wasn't until two years later, when Peggy was giving a talk, that I learned what a difference those brownies had made.

Peggy spoke about going through a terrible depression at that time. "I didn't feel that I was talented, or worthy, or even capable enough to have received this job as Relief Society president," she said. "I felt that the bishop had made a terrible mistake in calling me and that I was more or less an imposter. I was just waiting for others to catch on to my inefficiency." She had poured out her soul in prayer, asking for some reassurance—and that was the day I came by with my brownies.

Coming to Peggy's door with my meager offering was an answer to her prayers. Peggy began to realize that maybe she had made a difference, and that God was aware of her. A sweet peace came over her and calmed all of her fears. When I look back on this experience, I realize how both of us felt that we had not made a difference, when in reality we had done exactly that.

I've come to realize that when we are tempted to NOT do something, it is usually because it will make a difference for good in someone's life. I am so thankful that I listened to the Spirit that day and returned service to Peggy when she needed it most. The next time we feel the adversary's influence, we should get excited and know that something great is about to happen, because the adversary doesn't waste his time on anything unprofitable. We need to replace our fear with faith, and go forth and make a difference.

Katherine Harrison Ogden,
author of a book about singles

"Night Divine"

My heartstrings urged me to stay, though my head said otherwise. The Spirit had been shared abundantly, and we all had been spiritually fed. Now it was time for me to return home to my responsibilities as a wife and mother of five. What was keeping me here? Why couldn't I leave?

Earlier that day I had enjoyed speaking on the topic of service to a group of 150 missionaries from the Las Vegas Nevada Mission. I had admonished them to serve their companions, telling them that as they did, they would learn to love them. I shared the experience of a missionary who had come to our home, who was handicapped. It was difficult for him to talk, and many times he would trip and stumble when he walked. The compassion and service his companion gave him was immeasurable. Whenever this elder was having trouble eating, talking or walking, his companion was there to help him. He cared for him like the Savior would have. The effects of this love and service were felt throughout the area. They began to average three to four baptisms a month!

Several months earlier I had interviewed the mission president, President Ross McEachran, for a possible story for my book. I could see his mental wheels beginning to spin: He would extend the invitation to the missionaries to contribute stories if I would speak at their mission Christmas zone conferences. Excited at the possibility of having missionaries share their stories, I accepted. Little did I know that I would experience firsthand a story that would demonstrate one of the most Christlike acts of service and love I had ever witnessed.

We had spent the last two hours of the afternoon in a jovial manner. Holiday spirits were high as elders and sisters shared their talents with one another. They thoroughly enjoyed exchanging a few laughs, and the weight of missionary life was lifted from their shoulders for a few hours. The talent show was now drawing to a close. The skits from the various districts had been quite humorous, and a few musical numbers were sprinkled throughout the afternoon. But none could match the effect of one elder's rendition of "Oh Holy Night."

Elder Jones rose to his feet and walked to the front of the gym. He had been handed the microphone, but put it down because his hands were shaking so much. He looked out over the large audience and then looked upward as if offering a silent prayer. He took a breath, rearranged his shirt and coat, and then took another deep breath. He had my attention now! He made a few distorted facial features, followed by two more very deep breaths, as he stood silently in front of his peers. I couldn't imagine what he was about to do. At first I thought he was trying to get into character to perform a funny reading or something along those lines. But that was not it at all.

Very nervously, this elder began singing a cappella. The words he sang were very familiar. "Oh holy night, the stars are brightly shining. It is the night of the dear Savior's birth." A hush fell over the room. As the song continued and he climbed the octaves, his intensity grew and his face turned red when he tried to reach the highest strain, "Oh Night Divine." His entire body shook as he sang the last off-tune note, and the embarrassment I felt for him was overwhelming. The tension in the air was tremendous. "Thank goodness he made it through!" I groaned to myself. My heart went out to him, and I wondered how he was going to live down the ridicule from his fellow missionaries. As I breathed a sigh of relief that the song was over, he slowly began the second verse. I just about died! How could he go on? The paper he held in his hands now shook so violently that he could hardly read it. I could see the veins in his face protruding as he struggled to sing.

Then, as if out of nowhere, a Christmas miracle was born.

Somewhere in the crowd, an angel quietly began humming. At first it was so soft that it went unnoticed. Who was humming? It was so quiet that I wasn't sure what I was hearing; but soon the faint sound began to spread throughout the gym. The background humming gained strength until it became a perfect accompaniment for this struggling elder. I, too, found myself humming through my tears. I knew that had Christ been there, he also would have hummed.

When Elder Jones finished, I turned around to look at that blessed crowd of missionaries. The tears now came in floods as I watched these young messengers of Christ rising to their feet, giving a standing ovation to a fellow brother. Cheers, whistles, shouts of praise and encouragement rang through the room. I had been taught a perfect lesson of Christlike love and service.

Now I knew why I had been compelled to stay. What a wonderful Christmas present I had been given! I had never witnessed such an outpouring of love and kindness in my life. My heart was filled, and I could now return to my home with plenty to give. I had come to teach these missionaries how to serve, but instead I had been taught. Yes, it truly had been a "Night Divine"!

> Michele R. Garvin,
> mother of five, gives firesides on
> the subject of service

"Greater Love . . ."

"Daddy, Daddy! Tiffany is stuck on a rock and can't get down." The urgency of the child's voice indicated that the situation warranted immediate attention. Tom ran from the car and followed his child to the place where his daughter was hanging on for her life.

Earlier that day, my family and I had begun preparing the festivities for our youngest son's first birthday. All the normal celebrations were planned for that afternoon. It was during these preparations that I received a call on my beeper. I am a volunteer member of the Las Vegas Metropolitan Police Department Search and Rescue Team. As a member of this team, it is my responsibility to be on call and come to the aid of those in danger.

The urgent call indicated there was a nine-year-old girl stranded on a rock. I thought for a moment about the great distance—approximately 45 miles from my residence to this area. I decided that some of the other team members would probably be able to reach her sooner than I could; there were quite a few who lived much closer. I also hesitated since it was my son's birthday, and I continued with my planned activities. Only a few minutes had gone by, however, when I received a strong prompting from the Spirit telling me that I must respond to this call for help.

Not far from my home lived the Jackson family. Brother Tom Jackson and a few of his children had left earlier that morning for a family outing to the Valley of Fire, just outside Las Vegas. They arrived at one of the sites known as "Seven Sisters" about an hour later and began to hike the area and play on the beautiful red sandstone formations. The sun was bright and the steady beam had a relaxing effect on all of nature. Tom sat back in his car while his children played and he drifted off in a light slumber, until he was abruptly awakened by a call for help.

"Hang on, Tiffany!" he yelled as he quickly responded to her cries. To his horror, he found her poised on a vertical part of the rock, about 50 feet up the side of the formation. She was standing on a ledge only inches wide and clinging to a little knob on the rock just over her head. There seemed no possible way to reach her! A slight ramp in the rock led to within 15 feet of her location, but the space between the edge of the ramp and Tiffany's spot was divided by about eight feet of blank wall and a 40-foot drop. At the bottom were large, jagged boulders that would have caused serious injury or death if she fell.

Back in Las Vegas, after receiving such a strong prompting from the Spirit that I could not ignore it, I grabbed my uniform, told my wife I was leaving, and ran out the door. As soon as I logged on the radio, I got a call from one of the other team members who lived in the same end of town as I did. He asked me if I wanted to ride with him, since there was no reason for both of us to travel the distance in separate vehicles. That was the first time he had offered to drive to a call-out. Later I realized that this was the Lord working his miracles, through various people, to accomplish his purposes.

At the site of the crisis, as Tom reached the top of the ramp he realized there was absolutely nothing he could do to save his daughter. Yet there she hung, pleading for help. He had never felt so helpless. His daughter was out of reach, in extreme danger, and it seemed that all he could do was watch. At that moment, due to the fragile nature of the sandstone, the tiny ledge she was standing on crumbled and fell. Tiffany screamed, but held tight with her hands to the knot just above her, trying desperately to find some little outcropping where she could place her feet. With panic reaching a new level, Tom knew he had nowhere to turn but to the Lord. He said a short but mighty prayer, asking for help, pleading that his daughter would be saved from harm.

As soon as he looked up from his prayer, Tom noticed off in

the distance a small, green park-service pickup coming his way. He told his daughter to hold on, then raced down the rock formation to stop the truck. The driver was not able to personally do anything to immediately resolve the situation, but he had a radio and immediately contacted the park rangers. Within moments several arrived at the scene, only to realize that they did not have the equipment or the expertise to carry out the rescue. That is when they called the LVMPD Search and Rescue Team and requested their response as soon as possible.

Watching these proceedings, one of the park personnel stood at the edge of the ramp, staring in agony as Tiffany struggled to maintain her hold on the rock. It looked as if she would lose her grip any moment. Without warning or discussion, he leaped over the blank space in the wall and landed securely on a slanted outcropping just large enough for him to wedge his small frame into. From there he was able to reach up to where Tiffany was and brace one of her legs to keep her from falling. His position did not allow enough space for him to try to perform any type of rescue, but he was able to keep her from falling until further help could arrive.

During this time back in Las Vegas, I threw my gear in the back of my teammate's Suburban and we were off down the freeway heading toward the Valley of Fire. Hank had a reputation in the unit of being a very fast driver. I wasn't watching too closely, but I did notice that the speedometer stayed mostly on the far right-hand side of the gauge during our ride out there. Hank's was a speed I never drove, one that would normally make me very uncomfortable, but we arrived at the scene in just a little over twenty minutes.

It didn't take long to realize that the situation was desperate, and to understand why I had received that earlier prompting. I knew I would be called upon for service that day. Several attempts had been made by other team members to reach Tiffany, but without success. The Hughes 500F Helicopter from the Police Department had attempted to place someone on a ledge above her, but the rotor wash from the main blades was so strong that it almost blew her off the rock. One of the full-time police officers from our unit approached me and asked if I felt I could climb the rock face to the side of the girl, get above her on a ledge, and thereby effect the rescue.

During the past nine years I had been very active in technical rock climbing in and around the southern Nevada area. I was in good physical condition and well acquainted with problems and solutions associated with climbing on the different types of sandstone. Climbing in the Valley of Fire was something that was not done; the rock is so soft that often handholds and footholds crumbled when any weight was placed on them. Using the knowledge and experience I possessed, I had to decide if I thought I could climb the nearly blank piece of soft, vertical sandstone. There were no places available to place protection in case I fell. Other team members had already tried drilling and bolting, but the expansion bolts, once inserted into the soft rock, just pulled out again. If I climbed that rock, I would have to do it without any safety devices for my own protection. I took a few minutes to study the rock.

The words of a scripture (John 15:13) about laying down your life for a friend came to me. I had read this scripture several times, but it hadn't hit me with such impact until that moment. Christ had laid down his life for me. Could I do any less for someone else, someone in extreme need? Was this what was meant by "Christlike" service? Suddenly a calm, peaceful feeling came over me, assuring me that if I were to climb, I would be protected and no danger would befall me. I quickly grabbed my climbing shoes and other necessary gear and began the climb.

Each move was calculated. I found the strongest handholds, making sure my weight was transferred from hand to foot and vice versa very smoothly, one careful move after another, until I was even with Tiffany. Then, after a brief pause, I made the final move to the ledge above her. As I did, the rocks under my left foot crumbled, but my handholds remained strong and I moved to safety.

Within moments, I lowered a rope to another team member who quickly grabbed a harness and another rope. I raised him to Tiffany's level and held him tightly as he secured a harness and rope to her. After he was lowered, I tightly secured the rope which held Tiffany. For the first time in several hours, she was able to relax her hands and feet a little. "Tiffany," I said, "I need you to do something that may seem very uncomfortable."

With a frightened look she responded, "What's that?"

"Let go of the rock."

She was now forced to exercise the faith her father had shown when he asked for help from a loving God to save his child's life—but for her, it was faith in someone she didn't know. With trembling hands, she let go and put her faith in me and the rope I was holding. Within a few short moments I had lowered her to the top of the ramp, where other team members began checking for physical problems she might have suffered. To everyone's delight she was fine, and was soon in the arms of her father, sharing a loving embrace from him and other family members. I climbed carefully down the rock face, and the park-service employee who had risked his life jumping to the small outcropping was lowered to safety.

That day I went home feeling good inside. On the drive back, I thought about the events of the day. The decision I had to make was a difficult one, but I knew I had the skills and, with the Lord's help, could aid in the rescue. That part I knew. I thought again about what I said to that frightened girl. Then it was as if I could hear my Savior saying to me, "Marty, I need you to do something that may seem very uncomfortable."

I probably responded in the same unsure manner as Tiffany: "What's that?"

I could then hear Christ say, "Let go! I have paved the way for you. Lay your burdens at my feet and trust me!"

I have never felt so close to my Savior as I did that day. A new love for him engulfed my soul. "Greater love hath no man than this, that a man lay down his life for his friends." I was overcome with the deepest gratitude I had ever felt. "Thank you, Savior," I said, "my dearest friend."

Martin J. Rebentisch, serves
as a stake high councilman

A Guardian Angel

I watched with horror as the U-Haul truck my husband was driving sped off down the highway in an unknown direction. How was I going to find him again? I was almost out of gas. I had no major credit card, no checkbook, and only a couple of dollars. Our cash was with my husband, hidden in our suitcases in the back of the U-Haul.

Earlier that day my husband, Randy, and I had begun our move from California to Arizona. Randy was in the twenty-four foot U-Haul with our three-year-old boy as a passenger. I chose to drive our station wagon with my one-year-old son. Before we started our ascent over the Tehachapi Mountains, we stopped to converse about our plans for the night. Then with a kiss for luck, we were back on the road again. This was about five in the evening, and it was the last I saw of my husband until after a most unpleasant eight hours.

As we drove, a sign directed all heavy trucks to take another road. Randy took that route, but I didn't; I thought only trucks were allowed to access that detour. I didn't know where his road led, or if the route would rejoin the main highway. I had no idea how to drive through the maze of Los Angeles freeways, and I wondered if I should stop and call home. What if I stopped in a bad part of town? Would I jeopardize our safety?

Something whispered to me to stay on the road and follow the map I had tucked under the seat. I was to go to Indio; that was the only direction I could remember my husband giving me. So I drove on toward my goal in the desert, my baby squirming in his seat, tears rolling down my cheeks.

After dark, I exited Indio's first major off-ramp, hoping it was safe to do so. I found a telephone and called Randy's family. They had not heard from him and suggested I call the highway patrol. I searched the directory for the highway patrol office and called, praying that my husband had contacted them. Much to my disappointment, he hadn't.

I was also informed that I was in a bad part of town, and that I should go back one exit where I could find a decent motel. I quickly got back in the car, locked the doors, and proceeded to the motel. With my son in arms and looking quite disheveled, I descended upon the night manager. I pleaded with him to allow me to sit in his lobby until I found some way to contact my husband. I told him I had no money and nowhere to go. I'll never forget his compassionate look and gentle reply. "Of course, you can," he said with an understanding smile. What relief I felt!

The highway patrol finally provided contact with my husband. He should arrive in Indio, I was told, sometime after midnight. I collapsed in a chair in the lobby and wept. The night manager took me by the arm and placed me in one of his rooms. He brought me oranges and milk for my son, and told me I was to get some rest until my husband came.

Randy arrived later than expected, but what a joyful reunion it was! And that night, I came to understand the impact that one small, kind, seemingly insignificant deed can have. Because this hotel manager cared enough to help me through a terrifying ordeal, my son and I were safe, and my husband had a place to find me. This man who served me so well was my guardian angel for that night.

Peggy Ann Shumway,
mother of four active boys

Not Always Easy, but Worth It

"I'm losing her! She's falling!" Everyone was scrambling to hold her. We were in the rest room, quickly finding that there wasn't enough room for four people in a wheelchair stall. I was the strongest one there, so I put my arms under Carol's to help her onto the toilet. Multiple sclerosis had made her muscles work like jello, and Carol was starting to slip through my arms. I just knew she was going to end up on the floor.

Being a member of our ward's Relief Society presidency had proved to be very challenging at times. I remember that day ever so clearly. It was one of the last times Carol was able to come to church in her wheelchair. We had made it through Sunday School, and then suddenly she needed to go to the bathroom. As I was backing us into the special stall and holding her, the other two members of our presidency were trying to help, but were unable to do much.

We somehow managed to successfully complete the task, and I didn't lose her. However, by this time Relief Society had already started. The rest room was positioned right next to the Relief Society room, and there were no privacy doors between the two rooms to help muffle sounds coming from the rest room. As we walked into Relief Society late that day, the sisters' faces reflected pure compassion. I knew they had heard everything. It was a solemn day, and I was completely undone for the rest of it. Sometimes service is not only emotionally taxing, but also physically draining.

Several months earlier, Carol and her husband, an older couple, had moved into our ward. They lived twenty miles down the river. We were told something about their needs and asked if we, as a Relief Society presidency, could check on this couple. Carol and her husband lived in a tiny little camp trailer, with barely enough room for a table and a couch. At one end there was a kitchen and at the other end was a little bathroom and a bed. Her husband was doing the best he could. He planned to build a home for her on this property, but in the meantime they had to live in the tiny trailer.

When we first met Carol, we saw a very beautiful woman. I will always remember her fingernails—long and tapered and very delicate. Carol's condition was such that she needed to use a walker. MS causes the sheath surrounding the nerve in the spinal cord to deteriorate, and the body loses control of various motions and movements. The disease progresses to the point where the body finally shuts off and the person eventually dies.

Carol had suffered with this disease for some time, and was now having a very hard time getting around. When we would arrive, she would stand up to greet us by grabbing her walker. She could still walk, but her legs would go up and down in a springing motion. She looked just like a rubber band. It was hard for us to watch her lose the solid strength of her legs.

This illness also caused her to suffer tremendously in the heat. It was summer and very hot in that little camp trailer. There was an air-conditioner on the roof, so when she would get hot, we would turn it on. When she would start to get cold, we'd bundle her up. It was miserable for her; there was a very small range in temperature that accommodated her comfort zone.

Carol was not able to get into the bathroom by herself, and we discovered that she had no washing machine or dryer to wash her clothes as she soiled them. We would hand-wash her underwear and hang it out to dry. Then we would wash her dishes and try to figure out what we could get her to eat. She could not take a bath by herself or wash her hair. The day I washed and curled her hair, she was so happy and felt so much better about herself. As a presidency we took turns driving out to help her, which was about a 40-mile round trip. We spent many hours keeping her company and trying to help with her physical needs.

Something Carol desperately needed at this time was "in-home care." Many times a family needs help with this kind of technical legwork because they are often immobilized by the crisis. It consumes their emotions and energy, and they are unable to take the steps they need to obtain the services they are entitled to.

Our Relief Society president was an excellent example for us. We watched her dig in her heels and get these services for Carol. She went to every state agency, checking out all the services available to people with special needs, finding out who was involved, what the services consisted of, where they were, and how much they cost. This was not a simple thing. Finally she was able to get an agency called Chore-help to come and give Carol the daily care she needed. Her service of coordinating this care for Carol was so vitally important, her research invaluable.

Carol now is catheterized and has a feeding tube. The sisters still visit her on Sundays and sit with her so that her husband can attend church. They read to her and do other things to help her and to show their love.

This experience has helped me realize that Christlike service is not always easy or convenient. It took a great deal of time and energy to help this dear sister, many times sacrificing our own needs to aid her. The wonderful part about doing this was that we always left feeling better—that incomparable inward payment for serving others.

Sally DeSpain,
mother of four

Rufus

One day, a fifteen-year-old country boy came walking into Snowflake, Arizona. He was carrying a violin in a flour sack, with the bow sticking out of the top. He had no place to stay, no books, no change of clothes, and had walked more than 30 miles to get an education. Snowflake took him in. Someone gave him room and board, someone else bought his books. No one knew then that this country boy would change the lives of almost everyone who lived there.

Rufus Crandell graduated from the Snowflake Academy in 1910. After a year or two of teaching in normal schools, he went to BYU to pursue a musical career. In 1917 the United States was desperately in need of soldiers, and Rufus answered the call. He found his niche in the 158th Infantry Band cheering troops in France and England, where he received a shrapnel wound that gave him a limp for the rest of his life.

Following his discharge in 1919, Rufus had opportunities to perform with famous orchestras, but returned instead to Snowflake to teach music in the schools. Life seemed drab until he spotted a pretty first-grade teacher, LaVerne Richards. One day, four high school boys came into Miss Richards' room carrying a chair balanced on two poles. They asked LaVerne to sit in the chair, then carried her out past her amazed students, across the lawn, and over to the high school, where Rufus knelt and proposed to her. They were married in Salt Lake City, Utah, on October 4, 1922.

No children blessed the Crandell marriage, but their lives were filled with children. LaVerne was a great support to her husband, frequently offering her talents on the piano as Rufus molded bands, orchestras, choruses, glee clubs, church choirs, women and men's choruses, quartets, trios, and ensembles of every musical type and kind. People came from far and wide to take lessons. The *Messiah* was performed each Christmas with a full orchestra, chorus, and soloists.

Rufus began his career by teaching children in the elementary grades. For first-graders he'd play a note on his violin to start the singing. On Fridays he carried a record player, and the children listened to the classics. For third-graders he added more music and assigned each student an instrument. They met after school for band or orchestra, and Rufus gave each child weekly music lessons. My mother sometimes told me about many lessons on her borrowed cello. This was the Depression era, yet Rufus somehow found instruments for his children.

Fame could not help but follow such devotion. In time, Snowflake became known as the Arizona Salzburg, winning competitions all over the state. Its students carried on the tradition, spreading music wherever they moved. At a statewide music convention, Rufus Crandell was honored by the college music departments as the "Arizona Dean of Music," and lovingly called "that Grand Old Man of Music."

After nearly 50 years of teaching, Rufus retired, leaving others to carry on his tradition of classroom singing. If a teacher didn't have a background in music, she would exchange places with LaVerne or some other teacher so the music lessons could continue. A new teacher took over Rufus' high school work, but the school board couldn't find anyone who wanted to teach beginning instruments, so Rufus came back to teach the grade school bands and orchestras for several more years, with no pay. It was during these years that my parents moved back to Snowflake and I met Mr. Crandell. My family didn't have much money, but Rufus had an extra clarinet he let me use. He always seemed to have an extra instrument and a free lesson for the student who couldn't afford one.

I remember sitting in band and looking up to see this man's

scowling eyes, topped by large, bushy eyebrows, looking right at me. I was face to face with a legend, and my twelve-year-old ego was not comfortable. I had practiced my clarinet, but somehow it wouldn't stop squawking, and each squawk sent a scowl in my direction. Then an arm extended past those bushy eyebrows and calmly took my clarinet. Mr. Crandell began to play in clear and beautiful tones until the clarinet squawked again. Now he glared at it. "No wonder you can't play. I'll take it home and fix it. Can't have you playing like that." And so I learned that compassion lay behind those fierce looks.

Fixing a squawking clarinet wasn't enough for Rufus. He also gave me cello lessons, and his wife taught me to play the piano. Why? Was I destined for a great musical career? No. I was just one of the thousands of children and adults who learned to love music because the Crandells lived in Snowflake, served us all, and blessed our lives.

At age 68, that "Grand Old Man of Music" died of a stroke, but the real story of his music had just begun. Years later, after having been away for some years, my husband and I moved back to Snowflake with our young children. A new superintendent of schools had decided, because of limited funding, that some of the music teachers were expendable. The school size had increased, and only two music teachers had been hired to replace the four of earlier years. The superintendent did not know of the Crandell tradition, however, and a large portion of the town came out to a school board meeting to insist that a full music program remain in the schools.

Today, in my grandchild's first-grade class, a music teacher still comes into the classroom; perhaps he carries a tuning fork instead of a violin, but Rufus' influence is still felt. His music has been woven into the very fabric of our lives. We still have bands, orchestras, choruses, glee clubs, church choirs, women's and men's choruses, quartets, trios, and ensembles of every type and kind. Because of his legacy of music and the unlimited hours of service he contributed, people come from far and wide to participate in the outstanding quality of music performance offered in Snowflake, Arizona.

> JoAn Washburn, mother of
> eleven; author of Book of Mormon
> musicals

"Sacrifice Brings Forth . . ."

Is there ever a price too high to pay for desired blessings? The Lord promises that "sacrifice brings forth the blessings of heaven." However, it seems it is left to us to not only pay the price the Lord requires, but to understand what the currency is to be. The following personal experience and testimony are shared by Elder Gene R. Cook.

"In February of 1977, Elder James E. Faust, who was my Area Supervisor, came to Montevideo, Uruguay. While he was there, he received a call from President Spencer W. Kimball indicating that he and President Marion G. Romney would attend the ceremony for the laying of the cornerstone for the Sao Paulo Temple. Elder Faust was very enthused about it, and we were also, even though we could not attend. We were excited for the Saints in Brazil.

"At that point in time, the Uruguay/Paraguay Mission (of which I was president) and two stakes had gathered about 55% of their commitment towards the temple fund. The Saints had spent a year and a half arriving at that point. Elder Faust, in the presence of my two counselors in the mission presidency, said to me casually but full of faith, 'You know, it would really be a good thing if, on March 8, you could call Sao Paulo and tell President Kimball that all of the temple funds committed in your mission were gathered.' He didn't tell me to do it—he didn't even ask me to do it. It was a suggestion, but to me, a suggestion from a General Authority was a commandment.

"I remember that the first thought which came to my mind was the practicality of the situation. I knew where we were and how many thousands of dollars we were lacking. I also knew that the Uruguayan Saints had little money. I remember thinking, 'Do you know what you are doing? You are talking about gathering all that money in three and a half weeks.' And then very quickly came the Spirit to my mind, dominating the situation, and I said, 'Elder Faust, we will do it.' I asked my counselors if they were in agreement, and they were.

"Elder Faust left Montevideo a very happy man that day, but we were left with other emotions. He felt pleased. We felt a big burden. What were we going to do? We immediately knelt in prayer in my office. We talked of a plan. We determined among us that that was the will of the Lord and that we would accept it as such. He didn't tell us how to do it and we didn't ask—we just believed. I knew that first of all we had to be totally committed. I had given money to the fund previously and my counselors had done so on two different occasions. I said to them in the privacy of that meeting with just the three of us, 'Brethren, do you really believe that we can do this in three weeks? Let's be frank—*do you really believe?*' These were both good men and they felt the Spirit and said, 'We believe.'

"In order to act in faith, I gave them each a piece of paper and told them to write on the paper *how much they believed*, in dollars. Those good brethren each wrote down a figure. That was a real sacrifice for them—particularly to have to contribute again. The amounts were not great, but the *personal sacrifice* was.

"I knew that if those brethren and I were in tune spiritually as a presidency, things would be caused to happen. After that commitment had been made, I then read to them from the *Lectures on Faith* concerning sacrificing all you have and are and putting it on the altar of God, and said, 'Brethren, do you believe with all of your heart, and are you willing to give all that you have and are to fulfill that goal?' They both said that they did and were.

"I then committed them to this extent spiritually (knowing it would not work unless it were done purely by the Spirit): 'Brethren, I would like each one of us to commit, if you are willing, that one way or another, on March 8 the money will be paid even if it so be that the three of us pay it all.' Now the stakes were really high. They couldn't fulfill that commitment unless they sold every earthly possession that they had, and even then I am not sure that we would have reached it. But I wanted to know how deep their faith ran. Both of these men of faith, without hesitation, said, 'We commit to you, President Cook, and to the Lord, that the money will be paid. We have faith in the Saints that they will pay it, but if they don't, we will.'

"My counselors then left to do the work. *The spiritual battle was won. The spiritual creation in our minds and hearts was completely finished* with the finest of workmanship, even with finishing touches. For all intents and purposes, even the temporal task was done—we only lacked the *minor detail,* yes *minor detail,* of gathering the funds. As they visited district and branch presidents, could they testify of faith in the Lord? Sacrifice? Commitment? Yes, they could testify from the depths of their souls that this spiritual challenge was real. They did visit and in about two weeks, we had in our hands—after they had struggled previously for a year and a half—every single dollar and more.

"The next day, I took the two stake presidencies in Montevideo through the same process. The Lord provided the words.

"As the money, rings, watches, and even gold from the Saints' teeth began to pour in, my counselors and the two stake presidencies were overjoyed with the faithful response from all of the Saints, missionaries, and leaders. I am sure that this experience in the lives of the Saints prepared them spiritually to exercise faith, baptize hundreds, activate nearly two thousand people, and finally participate in the organization of four Uruguayan stakes on one weekend." (From "Faith in the Lord Jesus Christ," an address by Gene R. Cook. © The Church of Jesus Christ of Latter-day Saints. Used by permission.)

While the Lord does not always require us to give our *all,* under some circumstances much is required. May we be willing to sacrifice that which is needed in order to receive the crown laid up for us in heaven. "Therefore, O ye that embark in the service of God, see that ye serve him with all your heart, might, mind and strength, that ye may stand blameless before God at the last day." (D&C 4:2)

Story by Gene R. Cook,
member of the First Quorum
of the Seventy

Santa's Elves?

A load of sheetrock had just been delivered. I had been very busy, and I didn't see that it had been propped up against one of the walls. It was December 19, 1992, and my family was engrossed in working on our home, which was under construction. Later that day something was needed behind the stack of sheetrock, and it was moved slightly away from the wall. No one noticed the lurking danger this would later cause.

A loud thud, and then a piercing scream, echoed through the empty house. My blood ran cold. Instantly I knew what had happened, and ran upstairs to see my precious four-year-old, Audrey, lying underneath a thousand pounds of sheetrock.

After summoning help to free my daughter from her prison, we rushed her to the hospital. My poor little one's pain was so intense that she whimpered continually. After x-rays, the doctor explained that her femur had been broken near the hip. She was taken into surgery and a large, awkward body cast was placed on her. Anything but comfortable, it covered both of her legs with a bar joining the two, which prevented any walking. It also went across her hips and up underneath her arms.

Audrey was in the hospital for several weeks, and I stayed with her day and night to help comfort her. As Christmas approached, many wonderful people helped shoulder the responsibility of caring for my other seven children. My husband was a bishop at the time and helped as much as he could. We had already been through so much trauma, and the thought of not being together on Christmas was more than we could bear.

Early Christmas morning, at about 4:00 a.m., while Audrey was still asleep, I left the hospital to go home to be with the rest of the family while they opened their gifts. Later that morning the rest of the family came to the hospital, and we all were there while Audrey opened her presents. The children and I had really missed each other, and I was feeling the weight of being gone. Even though everyone took turns staying a day or two at the hospital, the burden was great. Tales from the siblings made it obvious that the absence of their mother was indeed being felt, and I hated to send my precious family home to be alone on that special day. They didn't even have a turkey to eat or any of the other special things I usually made for them at this holiday time. Our hearts were full, yet heavy, as we bade each other goodbye.

When the family returned home late that morning and walked into the house, they witnessed a small Christmas miracle. On our large dining room table lay an elaborate spread of holiday cheer—Christmas dinner at its finest. "Who has been here?" the children asked. "Was it Santa's elves?" one child asked. "No," their father replied, "but it was some of God's children commemorating the *true* meaning of this day."

As we all bowed our heads in prayer that night, Audrey and I in the hospital room and the rest of the family at home, we thanked the Lord for sending some of his angels that day to our home. Other Christmas days have come and gone since then, and I have realized what a busy, hectic time it can be. As I think back on that gift of timely, Christlike service rendered to us, I am reminded of the real meaning of that special day.

Name withheld

The Silent Strength of Others

A Parable

I was alone! All alone in the darkness of the freeway, going 55 m.p.h. I tried turning on the windshield wipers so I could see better and to help remove the rain that was now increasing. There was no action. They did not work. Then my headlights dimmed and, almost instantly, I was in complete darkness.

That day had started off fairly well. I had attended an excellent religion class at BYU where we discussed how the Savior taught the multitude in parables, which permitted him to teach "the mysteries of the kingdom of heaven" (Matthew 13:11) to those who would understand them. His parables had multiple meanings or applications appropriate to the spiritual maturity of the listener. They had a message for both children and gospel scholars. As I left the class, my mind was keen to the brilliance of the Savior's technique and I pondered, "How many modern-day parables happen right before our eyes, and yet we miss the great truths that have been taught?"

It was dusk, and I had been to the temple. As I got in the car to go home, I turned on my car lights without thinking. Then I remembered the problems I had with the battery after class, and I quickly turned them off again. Being a single mother brought with it many challenges. One of the hardest things for me was to have to rely on others for strength to help me out of problem situations. During the times my car would not start, I had been able to get jump-starts from other people. However, I felt secure now, thinking that the problem of dimming headlights had finally been corrected. I was truly grateful for a friend to drop me off at my car and wait to see if it would start. When the car started so quickly, I was confident that I would be able to get home safely, so I told my friend to go on home.

My feelings of security were a bit short-lived. It was dark and very late as I entered the south end of Provo. I became aware, once again, that my headlights were starting to dim. It was a fleeting observation and I did not dwell on it until I discovered that I was the lead car going onto the freeway at the University on-ramp. The curve was long and the street lights were not yet on. I was surprised when I realized that I could not see well enough to find the turn in the road. The reflectors on the side of the road gave me no feedback either. At 55 m.p.h. I didn't want to take chances, so I quickly put on my blinker and pulled to the side lane to let the other car take the lead. I pulled back into position behind him as I followed his car onto the freeway.

The rain began to drizzle a bit harder, and I noticed the lack of lighting on the freeway. I had driven this road many times, yet had never before noticed the lighting. I was thankful for the car that was leading the way in front of me, and I felt secure again. Then, without signalling, this car took the last Springville off-ramp. There were no cars in front of or behind me. I was totally alone.

"Oh, Father," I prayed, "please bless it to not rain any harder until I get home, and please bless me to get home safely." I soon noticed that the speed of the car and the wind action combined to remove the rain from the window, and I could see better. But now there was a more serious problem—a problem that if not corrected immediately would cost me my life! I needed to get a focal point, a distant object that I could use to determine my position, from which I could set my course. The freeway lights were not giving me any help, and there was no light from my vehicle for the reflectors along the side of the road to reflect back. I needed to find another source of longer lasting security, a source that would let me borrow some of its energy. But I could see nothing immediate that I could focus on or draw from.

The cars about two miles in front of me showed me that the highway was still straight. I followed in blind faith, relying on my memory; I had driven this same road hundreds of times. I prayed that there were no unseen obstacles in my path. I knew that other cars had also driven on this same road this same night, and they had passed through safely. This gave me courage to know that I could, too.

I was amazed at the total trust that was required. I seemed to be doing all right, but once again I turned to prayer: "Father, please give me strength to endure this emotionally stressful situation." I knew that if I stopped, I might give up the journey. If I slowed down, another car behind me might run into me from the rear because I had no taillights. My vehicle showed no visible signs to others that I was even present.

Before I knew it, I was in the freeway exchange at Spanish Fork. I had never before noticed such darkness. The freeway was curving, a gentle 90-degree turn that extended about half a mile. I could not even see the white line in the road, and the other cars were no longer visible. I had nothing to guide me through this turn, nothing except the distant lights of the town. I knew where I was, and I knew where I needed to go, but to what extent I needed to turn the wheel, I was unsure. Again I pleaded for help from the Lord: "Father, please help me to get through this area and this turn safely." I was ready to slam on the brakes right there. I was ready to give up. I wanted to stop. The unknown felt so unsafe. However, images of the distant cars in my rearview mirror made me feel that I would jeopardize their safety if I chose to stop now.

I drew upon the security of the distant lights ahead of me. I estimated the turn, and in the quiet darkness proceeded to do my part. I knew the Lord would do his. After going over the bridge, I could see a colored line in front of my car, about a foot to the right of my left wheel, pointing the way. Where was I? Was that the middle line? I looked again. No. It was a solid line. I had misjudged. I was way off course, about two inches from going off the left edge of the road. I quickly reevaluated my decision to use blind faith and decided that I needed help from someone else before I could go on. How could the Lord bless me if I did not help myself?

I pulled over to the side of the road, using the faint reflection of the distant lights upon the wet highway to show me where the edge of the road was. Carefully I pulled to a stop just beyond the Spanish Fork on-ramp. I thanked the Lord for blessing me to get through the last curve, and asked for another blessing to get home to my six waiting children.

It was not too long before a car came over the bridge. I quickly took my position behind this driver. He was going at a constant speed, not speeding up or slowing down, which gave me great security, and it was at a comfortable speed. I knew he was aware of my presence behind him, but I do not think he knew how much I needed his light and his silent support. There was such a contrast in how I felt now and how I had felt just ten miles back. I could very easily have gone off in the wrong direction and in a moment destroyed myself. Now I was secure and calm, following someone who had enough light to illuminate the road ahead for both of us. I was thankful for his preparation and for his presence.

When we turned onto the exit of my town, we pulled up to the stop sign. I wanted to jump out of my car and share with him what had just happened to me, and to thank him for his help and support. But as I approached his car, he turned the corner and was gone before I could get to him. He would never know of the invaluable service he had given me, the powerful influence for good he had been. I realize now, more than ever, that silent strength from others continues to see me through each day.

As I parked in front of my home and listened to the rain that was now coming in a heavy downpour, I realized that I had just experienced a parable. Just like Jesus's parables, it too had multiple meanings—great applications appropriate to the spiritual maturity of those who would receive it.

Carol Hill Curran Petersen,
currently serves as a
seminary teacher

No More Strangers . . .

The road seemed to narrow almost instantly, and directly ahead of us loomed a combine! This huge piece of farm machinery took up the entire road, leaving no room for us. I steered to the right, but there was no shoulder. The right front wheel dropped off the pavement, causing our car to roll several times out into the field.

It was in the late summer of 1952. The Utah fruit harvest was in full swing, and I had been doing a lot of peddling to various communities. Reed Bench, a good friend, had been with me for several trips, and we had decided to take a big load of tomatoes to Nebraska, where Reed's in-laws lived.

At the point of first impact, both Reed and I were thrown from the car (there were no seat belts provided in those days) and it was instantly flattened. As the first emergency team arrived on the scene, their first thought was that they would need the scoop shovels to pick up the victims, as there was RED all over! How relieved they were when they realized it was mashed tomatoes instead of blood! Reed's mother-in-law was a nurse and was with the ambulance team. It was a shock for her to find Reed lying on the ground in his injured condition.

At the hospital, Reed was diagnosed with internal injuries, a crushed cheekbone which required special care, a wrenched shoulder, and various cuts, scrapes, and bruises. I had a broken hand, broken ribs, an injured arm, and many scrapes and bruises. I had to spend more than a week in the hospital, and became as homesick as I was ill, being a typical sixteen-year-old. Family finances were very tight, but arrangements were made for me to travel home to Utah by overnight train, the best we could do for my comfort.

As I boarded the train, someone informed the porter of my condition and he said he would look after me. My ticket was for coach travel only, meaning that I would have to sit up, or only slightly recline, the entire trip—not a comfortable position for someone with broken ribs. After about an hour the porter, a large, friendly black man, told me I could move to any empty sleeper if I wanted to lie down. Even though I told him I could not afford the difference and would just stay where I was, the porter insisted. After helping me get to a sleeping room and bringing some extra pillows, he even brought me a lovely supper. Again I told him I couldn't afford it, but he just said, "Don't worry about it" and left the delicious-looking food. I had eaten hospital food for more than a week, and this food tasted just as good as it looked.

Through the night I rested fairly well, and the porter checked on me periodically. In the morning, he arrived with a tray of breakfast, again telling me not to worry about the cost. "Just enjoy," he said.

As the train pulled into the station at Salt Lake City, Utah, the porter arrived at my room with a wheelchair and helped me into the station to meet my parents. I fully intended to introduce the porter to my parents and get some money to tip the man for his kindness; but my parents were late arriving, and when I turned around, the porter had slipped quietly back to the train. I didn't even get his name! His care, concern, and service to me have made a lasting impression. This man, a stranger and a foreigner to me, exemplified such love and Christlike service. "Now therefore ye are no more strangers and foreigners, but fellowcitizens with the saints, and of the household of God." (Ephesians 2:19)

Carl Gurr,
serves with his wife, Edy,
as a full-time service missionary

"By Small Things . . ."

In only six short weeks, my life was to change drastically. My husband, Ralph, who we thought was so full of life and completely healthy, was diagnosed with a terminal disease. The doctors gave him six months to a year to live. We went into deep shock and felt that this was more than we could endure. We had been together only six years, and had looked forward to spending our later years together.

Twenty-five years earlier, Ralph and I had dated for a period of two years. We nearly married, but because of our age difference, we decided to go our separate ways.

A year later, I married a man who was to become the father of my two beautiful daughters. At the time it seemed right; however, when we moved to Las Vegas, things changed as he succumbed to the temptations of drinking and gambling. After trying hard to make it work, amid emotional and physical abuse, the marriage dissolved. During these miserable years I found the Church, which literally saved my life. As I learned of the truths the gospel taught, I had the courage to stick to my convictions, and I was blessed.

The year following my divorce, Ralph and I found each other again. It was amazing to see how Heavenly Father works in such mysterious ways and is personally aware of each of his children. It was no coincidence that Ralph chose this time for his retirement and came through Las Vegas. We were both guided by the Spirit to be in the same place at the same time so that we could meet once again. We renewed our friendship and found that our feelings, though long buried, were still very much alive.

Ralph told me that he would not make the same mistake he

had twenty-five years earlier and let me get away again. I told him that before we got too serious, I needed to share with him some of the changes that had occurred in my life while we had been apart. Ironically, at this same time, Ralph had been searching for the right church to join.

The mission leader in our ward commented that Ralph was the most "golden" contact he had ever met. He was not the type of man to do something just so he could get me to marry him; he was absolutely ready for the gospel. He took the missionary discussions, and ten days later was baptized. Six weeks later we were married civilly, and exactly one year later we went to the temple and were sealed. It was so wonderful to be happily married and have a spouse with whom I could share the same goals.

Several years earlier, prior to my marriage to Ralph, the Church had not allowed women to receive their endowments unless their husbands were also temple-worthy. I longed for the day when I could finally go to the temple and receive those blessings. I remember one Sunday when I was moved by the Spirit to stand and bear my testimony. I spoke of how it broke my heart to see that some members who had their recommends did not use them. I made the statement that I would give my right arm to be able to have a temple recommend; and if I had one, I would promise the Lord that I would use it.

In fulfillment of that promise, temple work became our focus after Ralph and I were married. Since Las Vegas didn't have a temple at that time, we purchased a motor home and drove up to the St. George Temple, completing five sessions a day from Tuesday through Friday for many weeks during the next six years. The temple became deeply important to us, and our hearts were full as we were able to serve the Lord in this capacity.

We were having the time of our lives; but it ended too soon. Just six weeks after being diagnosed, Ralph slipped beyond the veil with almost no warning. I began to feel overwhelmed by the responsibilities that lay ahead of me. It was at this time my dear friends came to my aid. So numerous were their acts of service and compassion that I still marvel at the outpouring of love I felt during this heartbreaking time.

It was the little things that touched me most. Ralph had died in his sleep in our bed. That same day, while I was making funeral arrangements, close friends came over and cleaned up. They put fresh, new sheets on the bed. That night, when I came home and was faced with the reality of Ralph's absence, one of these dear friends returned. She put me to bed and gently massaged my feet and legs until I was relaxed enough to fall asleep.

Others came to my aid as I tried to put my life back together after Ralph's passing. The Lord brought a new friend into my life with whom I shared my home; and through her, I met an angel named Ernie Atchley. He was so kind to help with things around the house, always there to fix and repair whatever was needed. No matter what problem came up, I knew I could call on Ernie and he would be there, never wanting to accept payment for his services. Sometimes he would show up even when I didn't ask him to—just to check up on things. Even now, at 80, Ernie serves two days a week as an ordinance worker in the temple. The rest of his time is dedicated to serving the widows, the fatherless, and anyone else in need.

During my years as a single sister, I experienced love and companionship as I shared my home with my new friend. For nearly five years we grew in the gospel as sisters, learning to serve each other. With the help and support of good home teachers and watchful care from Ernie, I felt the protective hand of the Lord in my life. I will never be able to fully express my profound gratitude for the true compassion and empathy I felt as a result of these small, but greatly significant acts of service.

> Barbara Kincanon Bindrup,
> serves with her husband as an
> ordinance worker in the Las Vegas
> Temple

It Came Naturally

Our house must have resembled an over-heated popcorn popper. When the rumbling and shaking didn't stop, we knew there were going to be problems. My wife, Patti, and I had enjoyed a peaceful sleep until we were jolted awake at 4:31 a.m. An earthquake registering 7.5 on the Richter scale had hit the Northridge, California, area on January 17, 1994, and we were right in its epicenter. We tried to get up and check on the kids, but couldn't find our shoes anywhere. We could hear glass breaking throughout the house and so were afraid to walk around in our bare feet. It was pitch black inside. The electricity had been cut off immediately, and there was hardly any moon that night. We couldn't see a thing.

Searching for a flashlight, we found nothing. We had tried to keep our flashlights hidden under the beds, but the kids always played with them. Our two-story house continued moving up and down and then sideways. We later learned that our house had moved two inches to the north on its foundation. I finally found some shoes and went to check on the children. Our two oldest had been awakened by the movement, and the baby was in his crib crying. Our nine-year-old had been sleeping on the top bunk and was really scared.

I made my way downstairs to look for a flashlight—Patti told me there was one in the pantry. I got there in time to see the entire contents of the pantry dumped onto the floor. It smelled like a Chinese restaurant, and I later found the reason—a bottle of soy sauce had broken and spilled everywhere. When I couldn't find a flashlight, I ran outside. I asked the first person I saw for his flashlight, and he immediately gave it to me. I was very moved that he didn't think of his own need first, but let me have it instead.

I quickly ran upstairs, and Patti and I gathered our five children and took them outside, where we huddled together. On the way out, we grabbed our coats and a pair of shoes for each child. We comforted each other and had a family prayer, thanking Heavenly Father that we were all right and had made it safely through this earthquake.

The neighbors had begun gathering outside, and we heard that one neighbor's gas main, two doors down, had broken. I immediately ran and turned our gas off. Then a neighbor and I knocked on doors to offer help in turning off others' gas mains and seeing if everyone was okay. At several homes no one came out, and we were worried about them; but soon all were accounted for.

I pulled my car out of the garage and then later went back and got our van. It had been on the side where much rubble had fallen, but I was still able to get it out. It was a blessing to have the van so Patti and the kids could sleep there that night. We live across the street from an elementary school parking lot, so we parked the vehicles there for the night. I left the family in the van and went to check on other things. Our dog was lost, and I was trying to keep an eye out for him. Later someone found him and brought him back home.

When first light appeared, a man that I home taught came to check on me. I was bishop of the Northridge First Ward at that time, and had just visited him in the hospital on Christmas Eve. I was deeply touched by his Christlike love, knowing that he was too sick to be out checking on us. He passed away before the end of the year, but his example continues to live on.

Members of the ward were so thoughtful as they tried to help ease our burden. After I made sure that my family was safe and taken care of, my next thoughts went to my ward members. Within two hours of the earthquake, a tent city had been set up on our Relief Society president's front lawn. I will always be grateful for Sister Doris Kilgrow's foresight.

My first counselor's home seemed to be the only one that had telephone service, and he and his family welcomed anyone who needed to use their phone. Later that day, several families exchanged things they needed with each other. One family had several lanterns and fuel, but no mantels. We had the mantels, so we shared; and both our families had light that night. The thing that amazed me was that for three or four days, no one was concerned about money or even going to work. The focus was on what was most important to us—our families and each other.

Our freezer was full of food, especially ice cream, because of an upcoming ward party. We had a big barbecue and served ice cream all day to anyone walking by. When tragedy strikes, it's surprising how it brings down existing walls. The older man next door who had never said hello, even when he'd pick up his newspaper, invited us to use the water from his swimming pool. Our water heater had broken and his son, a plumber, fixed it for free.

A Young Women's group in Orange County collected a tremendous quantity of helpful items. They brought these to us and we set them out on our patio. It was like a store, with diapers, water, food, and personal items available for neighbors and ward members. Many people in the "tent city" were very happy to have these items.

The most touching act of service we received was from a group of Primary children in the Salt Lake City area. A few weeks following the earthquake, a package arrived in the mail with letters from those Primary children written to the children in our ward. The letters were wonderful; they brought joy into our lives, and were the beginning of many pen-pal relationships which have extended to telephone conversations and even great friendships. What a blessing this little act of kindness has been in helping our children deal with such a major crisis.

As the week progressed, I was overwhelmed by the Christlike love and service that radiated from so many people. The general attitude of our ward members was utterly selfless: Once they knew they were safe, all they cared about was helping others. They didn't have to stop and think about what service to give— it just came naturally! Because I was listed as the bishop of the Northridge Ward in the general Church directory, I was inundated with calls. A group of Saints from up north called to say they had 100 people who could come at a moment's notice to help us. Another stake offered half a dozen plumbers. A Relief Society president from New York called to see if there was anything she could do. I was amazed at their charity! When the hurricane hit in Florida, I had never even thought to pick up a phone and call to offer our help. Through so many fine examples, I was taught a humbling lesson about Christlike service.

> Steven Duke,
> former bishop of
> Northridge First Ward

On the Lord's Errand

Money was rather tight, and I thought I could help if I found some part-time work. I read an ad in the paper that sounded like it might fit the bill, and soon I found myself attending a "group interview." By the end of the evening I knew that this job would not be our solution. However, during the break I visited with a young married couple who had just moved to our town. The wife was five months pregnant with their first child.

Once the interview was over, I told the young couple that while I was sure it wasn't their habit to ride with strangers, under the circumstances they might want me to drive them home. The husband hesitated, looked at his weary wife, and then accepted.

We chatted casually on the way to the apartment complex where they said they were staying with friends. I told them that after having five children, I had quite a few baby things I would be happy to give them. They seemed pleased and thanked me.

They requested that I drop them off in the parking lot. I asked them for a phone number so I could bring some baby things back to them. I wrote their number on a piece of paper, wished them well, and drove home to my family.

On the way home, I came to the conclusion that the reason I had been drawn to the interview was probably so I could help this young couple. As I told my husband about the events of the day, I received a very strong impression to prepare a "care package" of food for them. I felt there would be plenty of time later to get the baby things to them, but for now I couldn't ignore this prompting.

The following day I started working to put together the package. Our own cupboards were a little on the empty side as we waited for our next payday, but I gathered what I could. Then I called several neighbors and enlisted their help. Before long I had gathered four boxes of food and household supplies, including some delicious homemade bread and jam. It looked wonderful!

I called the number this couple had given me, only to find that the person who answered had no idea who I was talking about. "Well," I thought, "I must have transposed the numbers somehow. I'll just drive over there and find them."

Excitement ran through me as I thought of how thrilled this young couple would be to see all the food I had for them. Maybe I could even share the gospel with them. As I drove to where I had dropped them off, contentment filled my soul. It felt so good to be on "the Lord's errand."

The manager of the apartment complex refused to give me any information, which definitely interfered with my plans. Not to be dissuaded, I drove around the parking lot looking for this couple for nearly an hour. I prayed earnestly as I tried to find them. I even drove to a nearby shopping center and looked around.

My face was hot with tears of frustration as I finally pulled into my driveway. I told my husband of my efforts. He said not to worry about it, I had done my best. But I knew the Lord had TOLD me to prepare this care package, so I insisted that my husband help me try to find them. Because of his love for me, he drove me back across town.

We had about the same experience together that I had had on my own. I couldn't understand it. Why would the Lord instruct me to put together this food, and then make it impossible to deliver?

Jim and I drove home in gloomy silence. We had no sooner pulled into the driveway than I had a new surge of hope. My husband stayed home this time, but I drove back across town yet another time. I was convinced that this time the Lord would help me find "my" couple. No such luck!

Parked by the side of the road, tears streaming down my face,

I pleaded with the Lord. "I KNOW that thou instructed me to put together this food!" Then, ever so quietly, a clear voice came into my heart and mind, saying, "Yes, my daughter, I instructed you to put together this food. Now, be still and I will tell you who it is for." I was shocked. Instead of being so frantic to do what I thought was most important, I sat quietly. Almost instantly the name of a couple, our very good friends, came into my mind. I knew that they had been struggling, but it hadn't occurred to me to take them anything special.

I drove slowly home, then gave my friend Louise a call. "Louise, this is Stephanie," I said. "This may sound strange, but I have several boxes of food in my trunk, and I think they belong to you."

Stunned silence. "What did you say?" she cautiously asked.

"Well, I felt impressed to put some food together today, and I think it's for you," I repeated.

"Just a minute," she replied. She was gone from the phone for a couple of minutes. When she returned, she told me that she had had to stop her husband, who was on his way to the store with their tithing money. They had been out of food for a couple of days, and had finally decided to use the only money in the house to buy food.

As I joyfully drove to my friends' house, I reflected on how, in our eagerness to be "on the Lord's errand," we sometimes actually get in his way. The Lord had told me to put some food together, but I was the one who had decided it was for the elusive couple. The Lord had other plans. In my determination to do what I thought was needed, I almost missed a wonderful opportunity to bless the lives of some very dear friends.

The words of a very familiar scripture came to mind: "The Lord giveth no commandments unto the children of men, save he shall prepare a way for them that they may accomplish the thing which he commandeth them" (1 Nephi 3:7). It all made sense now. The Lord had used my service to prepare a way for this family to accomplish the thing which was commanded of them. I felt truly humbled to have been an instrument in his hand.

Louise met me at the door with a hug. Then, arm in arm, we went to my car to bring in the food the Lord had wanted them to have in the first place.

Stephanie Abney, mother
of five, serves as a
stake missionary

Who is My Neighbor?

The days were getting longer and hotter, and the last of our visiting "winter residents" were heading home. Here in Mesa, Arizona, we have fabulous winters, but our summers are hot enough to send anyone packing.

I was coming home from work when I first noticed him—a tiny, older man parked on the side of our street. He towed a second car, and both cars were filled to the brim. The cars' license plates indicated he was from Canada. The hood of the first car was raised, so I pulled up alongside him and asked if he needed help. "No, thanks," he said. "Everything will be fine." So I went home.

The next morning, the cars were still there. He was out of his car tending to a couple of dogs that were traveling with him. I dashed back home and returned with a jug of cold water and a bag of grapes. I wished him a safe trip, as I was sure he'd be gone by the time I got home from work.

I was wrong. By afternoon, he was still stranded. This time I stopped, got out of the car, chatted with him, and met his dogs. His name was Pete. He didn't seem to have much money and most of his worldly goods were in his two old cars, both of which were now disabled. I admitted to him that while I can fix nearly any appliance or do any household repair, I didn't fare too well when it came to cars. Apparently, he didn't either.

Pete did not go unnoticed in our neighborhood. Several men had been by and poked around under the hood of his car, all with no success. The third day came and went, and Pete was still stranded. My wife took him some cold water and more fruit. Once again, he spent the early summer night sleeping in his car with his dogs.

On the fourth day, the manager of the "Whataburger" brought him a burger, fries, and a drink. We tried to keep him supplied with cold water and fruit, and we invited him to the house for dinner and/or a shower. He was timid and worried about his dogs. He said, "No . . . thanks."

I stopped briefly to visit with Pete on the fifth day and slipped him a twenty-dollar bill. He was grateful and slightly embarrassed, but I was glad to help in any way. I wished I knew more about car engines. It was obvious that Pete barely had enough money to get home, and he certainly couldn't afford to hire a mechanic.

I knew of only one person with the expertise to fix Pete's car—my good friend, Fred. If Fred couldn't fix a car, no one could. Pete couldn't afford to pay Fred anything and neither could I, but I knew that wouldn't stop Fred from fixing Pete's car. He regularly fixed cars for friends just for the cost of parts. He had a big heart—but he also had a large family, and one of his daughters was getting married soon. He had relatives visiting. How could I possibly intrude on Fred's precious time? No, this wasn't his problem; he didn't even know Pete. I decided not to involve Fred.

Neighbors continued to try to be helpful, but it wasn't enough. Pete had been stranded on our street for a total of ten days, and his situation was looking rather hopeless. It had gone on too long. Finally, I called Fred.

With no talk of money, and his daughter to be married early the next morning, Fred came out to fix Pete's car. Neighbors came by and told Fred all the things they had already tried without success; they told him the car was too far gone. But not for Fred. In less than an hour, he had Pete's car humming. With tears of gratitude and relief Pete thanked Fred, who made a quick exit back to his busy household.

Once again, I invited Pete to our home for a meal and a shower. Soon there was a quiet knock at our door. I opened it and there stood Pete. Although he refused dinner, he had some fresh clothes tucked under his arm and was looking forward to getting cleaned up.

Pete soaked in our bathtub for nearly an hour. Afterward, he sat down and visited with us. He noticed pictures of the Savior, the temple, and the First Presidency on our wall. We told him we were LDS and explained a little bit about our church. He said he had driven by an LDS temple in Canada. Through the evening, Pete thanked us several times for our help. We assured him that we could not have done it alone.

As I drove down our street the next morning, I glanced over to the left, expecting to see Pete with his dogs and cars. I felt a little twinge as I looked at the empty spot where he had taken up residence the past ten days. But now he was gone.

That night as I read my scriptures, I came across Luke 10:27: "Thou shalt love the Lord thy God with all thy heart . . . and thy neighbour as thyself." Continuing, the scripture asks, "And who is my neighbor?" Pete is my neighbor. He's Fred's neighbor, too. And for just a little while, we were privileged to serve him.

Jim Abney, serves as
a Blazer teacher in Primary

A Soul in Need

I picked up the phone to hear the moans of a very sick-sounding woman. "Michele," she groaned, "I'm feeling awful!" At first I was caught off guard, but then I asked her what I could do to help. She quickly replied, "I need you to come over and do my dishes."

This was during the first few years of our marriage, when my husband and I were knee deep in work, school, and church. Craig was incredibly busy—working full time, going to school full time, and serving as the elders quorum president. While I stayed at home with our two small children, I also did typing for small businesses. We both did janitorial work and odd jobs so we could financially survive during those hard years.

During this time I had been assigned to visit teach a young woman named Kim. She had married quite young and already had several children. She hadn't learned how to make friends very well, because at times she could be downright obnoxious. On this particular day, I received an urgent call from her—to do her dishes! I couldn't help wondering how many women would have loved to have someone do their dishes, but didn't have the nerve to ask. I imagined that she must be deathly ill in order to ask me to do that. I could picture her kitchen sink heaped full of dishes, and my heart went out to her. But her next words caught me off guard: "I'm so sick that I'll have to ask you not to bring your children." I later found out that she had someone else watching her own children.

At this time in my life, a babysitter was like gold. We didn't have any extra money, and the only time we used a babysitter was when we went to the temple, for our anniversary, or for something really special. So for me to go wash someone's dishes, and get a babysitter too, seemed to be service above and beyond the call. I chastised myself, realizing that service is not always convenient and we need to serve when others are in need. With that in mind, I relented and got a babysitter.

As I entered Kim's home, I found her lying on the couch. Her feet were kicked up, and she was watching TV and eating bonbons. No, not really. But to me, she didn't appear sick! Nevertheless, I thought I'd better give her the benefit of the doubt. I sat and visited for a few minutes until I became a little fidgety. I wanted to dig into the dishes, but she didn't seem concerned with them at all. I tried to get up several times, but she just kept talking.

Irritated, I was finally able to tear myself away from the couch and get to the task at hand. I had envisioned piles and piles of dirty dishes, but when I walked into the kitchen I was not prepared for what I saw. There on the table were four paper plates, four cups, a pizza pan, and a pot for vegetables. There were only a few other dishes in the sink. Immediately my anger flared. "This is what she called me over here to do, and there sits my expensive babysitter!" I couldn't believe it. I grudgingly started cleaning off the table and doing the trifling work before me, all the while wallowing in my own negative attitude.

As I stood at the sink, I seemed to hear my mother's voice from years past: "Michele, when you do service with a bad heart, it's as if you didn't even do it, and it is counted against you. 'For behold, if a man being evil giveth a gift, he doeth it grudgingly; wherefore it is counted unto him the same as if he had retained the gift; wherefore he is counted evil before God' (Moroni 7:8)."

I looked down at my watch and thought, "Okay, you have just wasted half an hour! Straighten up, and serve with the proper attitude." As soon as I altered my thoughts, an actual change came over me. I started feeling toward Kim as Christ would have, and suddenly I felt like I loved this sister.

At that point, I noticed other things that needed attention. I went through her house and started cleaning, and she let me.

Then I did her laundry, and she let me do that, too. Then I sat down and began visiting with her, and it was obvious that she wanted me to stay. This is when I learned a most important lesson about ministering to a "soul in need." This dear sister's needs went much deeper than concern over a few dirty dishes. Once I straightened up my attitude, I was able to focus more on her less obvious needs. Her call for help had nothing to do with the dishes. Because I finally listened to the Spirit and began to share myself with her, I was able to fill a much greater need—friendship to her soul.

Michele R. Garvin,
serves as a visiting teacher

About the Author

Michele Romney Garvin is a woman of many talents and interests. Among her favorite pursuits are speaking, songwriting, reading, writing, swimming, sewing, volleyball, family reunions, and husband/wife getaways. She enjoys sharing her talents and has given firesides in Arizona, Nevada, Utah, and California. She loves speaking to the youth, but has also spoken to many adult audiences.

Service has always played a great part in Michele's life. She wrote her first song, "The Law of the Harvest," in 1990. This special song about service was inspired by the example of her parents, George Lee and Pearl T. Romney. She has recently written another song, "The Miracle of Service," which was inspired by the compilation of this book.

Michele and her husband, Craig, live in Las Vegas, Nevada with their five children. She has served as a teacher and music chorister in every Church organization; she has also participated in many choirs and loves sharing these talents in her ward and stake. Michele has also served as an activities chairman and Primary president, and currently serves as activities chairman in her stake.

Special Note

Sister Garvin continues to speak, write songs, and collect stories about service. If you have a story you would like to share, you may contact her at the following address or phone:

Michele R. Garvin
4979 Tee Pee Lane
Las Vegas, NV 89129
(702) 645-8251